Judy Gleason

A Woman For All Seasons

A Woman For All Seasons

by
Jeanne W. Hendricks

THOMAS NELSON INC., PUBLISHERS
Nashville / New York

ISBN 0-8407-5630-5

Table of Contents

Dedicated to Howie,
whose lifetime of love has tutored me
in the rewards of womanhood

Preface

Until recently it was a simple matter to be born a girl. A bit plebeian perhaps, but uncomplicated. There were cultural pigeonholes, and with few exceptions society placed you there with or without your consent. You may have pouted, scratched, and screamed at the nutrition and needlework routine, but that was your label, whether you wanted it or not. You were a girl; *ipso facto*, your life was to consist of cooking, sewing, bearing babies—all with open-ended opportunity for such menial chores as were applicable.

Present-day pigeonhole painters have been offering variations of girl places in the human nest. For several decades, dark clouds of questions about women have been growing more threatening. Like descending tornado funnels, some of these dilemmas have pierced our routine of living. The feminist movement has marched into our lives, turned homes inside out, and propelled women into such male sanctuaries as the executive board room, police patrol cars, and even the astronaut program.

Zooming in the opposite direction, a small book called *Total Woman* reached unprecedented heights of prominence by advising wives to submit to their husbands. Debaters, lecturers, and playwrights have tendered a literary smorgasbord to delight every taste on the subject of the female.

It is impossible to hide our heads in the sand or put on generic ear muffs. The sirens are screaming that we simply must not dress little girls in pink and boys in blue, buy our babies "sexist" toys, or let them learn to read Dick and Jane. Whether it's housework or soccer, we must all learn to do it; if we ever get turned down for a job because of our brand of hormones, it's a federal offense.

All these no-no's and go-go's have created a monstrous complex of confusion, especially for women. A man can largely take it or leave it, but a woman faces personal decisions every day, policy decisions that hang on a nagging question—is it really right?

In her brilliant assault on the Lib Movement, Ariana Stassinopoulous *(The Female Woman)* declares, ". . . the truth will make you free, but only if you have a way of ascertaining what the truth is." I have dug into the historical bottom of the pile in order to ascertain the truth from the past to clarify the present. As great as it is, the story of women is more than suffragettes parading in Washington and women voting in 1920. Or forty years before that, when Belva Lockwood scandalized gentility by whizzing through the capital on her tricycle to dramatize the petticoat vote issue. This was but one chapter in a long history of reforming legal deficiencies.

A tortuous fight raged much earlier in an effort to rectify educational imbalance. It was 1789 when Boston began allowing girls to go to school. But while some of the earlier humanists and even the sage philosophers, Plato and Seneca, recommended intellectual grooming for women, only a very select number of women of the court ever realized this privilege. No matter how far back one delves, women have been cradled in the question of social issues.

Flip over to the present scene. The 1976 report of the Commission on the Status of Women in my own city shows that 14 percent of the families are headed by women.* Gross inequality in pay scales exists: the average salesman earns $10,000 annually, contrasted with the average saleswoman's $3,800. In our city governmental structure there is neither internal career development nor management training for women. The most serious problem of the year was rape, with only one case in ten reported. Less than one in four of the women in this wealthy, progressive city have attended college.

Such statistics surprise very few thinking people. But the process of upgrading women seems to move in one direction only—legislation. Force the legal door open. Demand equality. It is a cold, steely gleam of aggression that shouts in the words of Gloria Steinem: "No one will give you power or equality. You have to take it!"

Do we? "All authority has been given Me in heaven and on earth," says Jesus Christ (Matt. 28:18). He alone dispenses influence, dignity, and rightful power. He has a workable plan for women, and it is always in a cooperative relationship with men, never in ill-matched conflict. Will we have to say at the end of the century, "The operation was a success, but the women died"?

To look at our late twentieth-century world, we might conclude that God had never spoken on the subject of women. But He did—definitively. Not in a

---

*Nancy Smith, "Profile of the Dallas Woman," *Dallas Morning News*, Jan. 11, 1977.

list of rules, but in selective reports of women who actually lived in diverse cultures—reports which prove God has not overlooked the females. Only we have missed His message.

How far back shall we go for answers? Let's go to the beginning. The historical, interpretive record of the Bible illuminates the winding path of women through the centuries. The Bible is not primarily about women. It is the record of God's plan to rescue all persons from the impossible sin predicament. Pathos and suspense clothe the characters; the knowledge that these people are real and the facts are history bring it alive. What God has to say about women becomes *raison d'être* in whatever case we construct for the female sex.

Since my world seems to be divided on the subject of where I fit as a woman, I want the directions from the Manufacturer which, undoubtedly, were quite clearly understood when the first model was marketed in the garden of Eden.

A kind of archaeological dig is possible through the sacred Scriptures from the dawn of history through to the early Christian era. Like pieces of perfectly preserved pottery, each woman reveals a rich vein of information—cultural characteristics, personal quirks, and more importantly, the constant factor of the divine commentary.

Marriage, motherhood, widowhood, royalty, and more. God has case histories, complete with editorial comment, on women in all slots of life. A close scrutiny of what He says is like finding answers in the back of the book. Womanhood suddenly makes sense and becomes a priceless privilege.

> Jeanne W. Hendricks
> Dallas, Texas

A Woman For All Seasons

1
Three Phases of Eve

Somewhere between the sophomore daze and the senior semi-ignorance of my high school career, I began to see myself as a woman. Like the famous little "engine that could," I was beginning to puff up a head of steam as I struggled up the hill toward adulthood: "I-think-I-can, I-think-I-can. . . ."

The national mood was militaristic. In the wake of Pearl Harbor every man, woman, and child was expected to pitch in and help fight "the enemy." I hurried as fast as possible to tear off the togs of childhood and climb into adult robes. Finally, exhilarated with the hauteur of a diploma, I willingly postponed higher education and signed on with a large company to type lengthy requisitions for eight hours every day.

"This is the *real* world," my family and friends assured me. With high hopes I became a daily straphanger on a crowded trolley car rattling toward center-city. At the office I became acquainted with the files and the people and the machines—all pretty much alike. I learned to live with the choking cigar smoke from my supervisor across the aisle. With timing and speed I could dodge the foreman who made passes at me, when I went into the stock room for supplies. The job settled into a routine of daily doings with few headline features. The world, I learned, had a deadening sameness about it that wore people down to autistic blobs.

At a Christmas dinner, where attendance was mandatory, I discovered the office people had a baudy sub-layer. With a little liquor the men unleashed an ugly machismo and the women became wanton coquettes. Fortunately, I had to leave early.

Not too many months later the personnel manager narrowed his eyes and looked at my resignation form I had brought to his desk. "You're probably making a wise decision," he said flatly. "You really belong in college. Good luck."

I cleaned out my desk and took the elevator down to the noisy street for the last time. I had wanted so much to be a part, but I was on a different wavelength. Why? My questions were unformed, but they were pricking inside my head.

Were the preachers really right, that a woman's place is in the home? Is a woman, after all, really meant to be the plaything of a man? Why has God given me this geyser inside, this irrepressible desire to learn about things and people and the answers to riddles? Some of the answers came when I visited the Garden of Eden via the book of Genesis.

The Perfect Triangle: Adam—Eve—God

The garden of Eden houses a well-packed parachute out of which streams all of history, science, "ologies," and "isms" known to man. Life in the garden is more than just an intriguing story of God's fashioning a woman to integrate the life of the first man. It is more than just a dramatic scenario from the ancient past. Thereon hangs not a *tale* but a *trail*, a path that leads right to your front door—and mine.

With this single exception of Eden, beginnings have always been hard. I remember reading about the first two white women on the Oregon trail.

Back in the 1830s there came to Fort Vancouver a medical doctor and a Presbyterian minister, Marcus Whitman and Henry Spalding. Their wives, lovely blonde Narcissa Whitman and tall, dark, beautiful Elizabeth Spalding were both new brides traveling west for their honeymoons. They had to discard their precious possessions one by one to lighten the load on the overtaxed draft animals. Finally they had to cut their covered wagon in half, and they reached Idaho in a rickety two-wheeled vehicle. They barely made it to Oregon on horseback. Six months after they arrived, Narcissa was delivered of the first white American child born west of the continental divide.[1]

Honeymoon Hideout

In contrast, the Genesis beginning was housed in perfection for Adam and Eve. Life was genial. First, let's pick up the weather report. "But a mist used to rise from the earth and water the whole surface of the ground" (Gen. 2:6). The honeymoon cottage had an automatic sprinkler system!

It also had an eastern exposure. The morning sun came into the kitchen. "And the Lord God planted a garden toward the east, in Eden; and there He placed the man whom He had formed" (Gen. 2:8).

The job outlook was bright. Adam was employed with a rather creative and fulfilling profession.

"And out of the ground the Lord God formed every beast of the field and every bird of the sky, and brought them to the man to see what he would call them; and whatever the man called a living creature, that was its name" (Gen. 2:19).

Eve had it made. She was even spared the pain of growing up. When God created Eve, she had—to put it in our vernacular—the whole ball of wax, a winning hand.

Move in for a close-up view. In the original Hebrew, God used two different words to describe the creation of Adam and Eve. In creating the man, the ordinary word for "making" is used, such as one would use to describe the molding of a clay pot. In the description of Eve's appearance, however, the word is "hand-crafted," or literally "built." "And the Lord God fashioned [built] into a woman the rib which He had taken from the man, and brought her to the man" (Gen. 2:22).

There is a noticeable holy hush over this incident. It stands in sharp contrast to the coarseness and irreverence in which modern life is packaged. The silence seems to signify a kind of historical fulcrum, for with Eve the pulse of humanity begins to beat. You can see it coming in the words of the Creator, "Then the Lord God said, 'It is not good for the man to be alone; I will make him a helper suitable for him [or "corresponding to" him]' " (Gen. 2:18). Jehovah spoke. It was the first time He had said anything was *not* good.

Phase I—Morning of Purity

Jehovah God never wastes words, never indulges in idle prattle or useless thinking. There is no secondary level of importance to His communications. He spoke, and He said that it *was not good* that man should be alone.

Alone? With every animal on earth a personal friend, subject to his every whim, responsive to his commands? Alone? With God Himself coming to call?

Alone. Because he himself was incomplete, unfinished for God's purposes. A vacancy existed in his personal experience.

Notice that God did not make another man to fill the void. He did not need an apprentice in the garden, or a colleague to help catalog animals. He was performing his job adequately. Adam was no under-achiever, but his need was singularly private.

Adam's lines of communication moved upward to His Maker and downward to the earthly plants and animals, but there was no reply to a horizontal message. He may have noticed how each animal sent out its mating call—and received a response.

I remember well touching the sensitive nerve of a common wavelength deep inside myself and my Howie before we were married. As teen-agers will, we were discussing guys and gals, marriage and future dreams, all interlocked with the tidy idealism that erects castles in the air. My memory refuses to play back an exact recording of his statement, but he told me with high-voltage intensity how much he honored and respected and loved one person—me. That statement, now reinforced with more than thirty years of knowing him intimately, propelled me into a flight pattern in which I still soar. No other human experience quite equals the certainty that you are the one and only lifetime choice of your partner.

Adam, of course, did not make that choice; God made it for him. And I believe with all my heart that God also made it for my husband. Experience has convinced me that we humans are not really smart enough to choose mates. One big reason is that we simply cannot see the future.

This man Adam was made to love another like himself, to share this Edenic life, to laugh, to dream, to find completeness in another person. Without Eve, God's creation was not yet finished. He had crowned the magnificent progression of animal life with the making of a man, a unique creation fashioned on the pattern of His own likeness. Adam was a reflection of His own glory, made with the ability to know and understand something of the heart and mind of the eternal Jehovah God. Now He would crown this man-reflection of Himself with yet another reflection.

Even as Adam portrayed God's glory to the earthly habitation, so this new creature would interpret Adam. She would provide the extension of Adam's self in sensitive paths where He could not go. She would make him a whole being, add the dimension of full, rounded satisfaction to his life. She would furnish the means to produce more individuals to populate the fresh new earth.

"Ugh! Eve was made from one of Adam's spare parts, almost as an afterthought to help him out on earth!" spewed one disoriented female.[2] "God created woman . . . and from that moment boredom ceased. And many other things ceased as well. Woman was God's second mistake." So snorted Frederick Wilhelm Neitsche.[3]

Derailed, deluded, modern man would discredit God's holy purpose. Is this Old Testament narrative genuine, he asks. Or is the creation story a fake, perpetrated on us by some clever old Jewish story teller? We will assume and rest out eternal destiny on the fact that this scenario really happened. A sparkling thread that attests to authenticity is spun into the precepts of Moses, the prophets, the evangelists of Scripture, even affirmed by Jesus Christ Himself. On through the teachings of the church fathers, the conclusions of brilliant thinkers such as Blaise Pascal, the poetry of John Milton, the precise deliberations of John Newton, and an innumerable host of others. Many have staked their lives on the veracity of this Word.

Meanwhile, back in the garden, who was the new woman on the scene? Fortunately, we have an eyewitness account. God gave her the finest welcome any debutante ever had. Remember when God brought her to the man, this brilliant intellect, this executive over the whole complicated earthly system? Immediately he responded, "And the man said, 'This is now bone of my bones, and flesh of my flesh; she shall be called Woman, because she was taken out of Man' " (Gen. 2:23).

Identity

The first thing Eve received was an identity. The Hebrew says literally, "this one at this time. . . ." Dr. Francis Schaeffer points out that this designation gave the historical emphasis.[4] The expression was one of excitement and enthusiasm, "Here now at last!" Jesus Christ confirmed this event centuries later (Matt. 19:4). She was what she was because she was taken out of man. One man and one woman—a complete unit.

Relationship

"I have been waiting for *you*." That is the thought behind Adam's initial words. What sweeter sound could she have heard? Not only does she learn she is a full-fledged person, but she is in a relationship. Adam observed that her bone and her flesh matched his own—physical compatibility. Not only did she match; she was *part of him*. He understood what God had done. No need to elaborate on the closeness of physiological kinship. "When it comes out of my body, it's special," Adam thought. "I have a possession I want to protect, for which I make provision."

Marriage in a Nutshell

"For this cause a man shall leave his father and his mother, and shall cleave to his wife; and they shall become one flesh" (Gen. 2:24).

In a flash of brilliant insight, the first man set the course of sociology. A tripartite pronouncement: He was to break a relationship he himself had not experienced (parent-child), to form a new unit of society, and to engage in a unique blend of interpersonal mating. One person plus one person equals one person.

All the pleasant, stimulating botanical and zoological studies which Adam had enjoyed—even the exquisite communion with God Himself—could not do for this man what this new person could. Adam must have looked at the woman from head to toe, talked with her, and bubbled over in a crescendo of joy. There is no hint that Adam sensed "now my troubles are beginning," or that he suspected God had subtly foisted on him a burden. Eve was not an additional job assignment. Adam understood clearly and he was elated.

As the wife of a professor in a graduate school, I am privileged to see close up many newlyweds who arrive on campus at the beginning of each school year. It is a particular delight to observe a few young husbands who never get over the thrill of their special hand-picked wives. All the pressures of assignments and exams never seem to dim the glow in their eyes when they look at their wives. I feel sure Adam glowed like that.

So God created a married couple. Interesting, isn't it? The holy state of matrimony—trampled and degraded in man's schemes—glistens as the crowning jewel of the perfect creation. One can only imagine the marvelous details of their wedded bliss. Did God whisper any premarital instructions to Eve? How did He prepare her for her wifely responsibilities? We cannot know all the delicate inner lining of Eve's "phase one." We do know she flourished in a union legally sanctified and secured by the Judge of all the universe.

On this historical base I, Eve's daughter, can place my own identity. I know who I am, and how I am made—in the image of God. That fact gives me reverence and respect for my body, my mind, and a clue for my eternal destiny. It tells me God is relational. As I learn to know Him, I can reach out to others. My life has meaning and purpose.

Phase II—Spiritual Suicide

Eve—and history—turned a sharp corner in a flash. The serpent hissed and Eve's "phase two" inverted paradise. A mere question, quivering like the jab of an anesthetic needle, pierced her innocence. She toppled helpless, unsuspecting before her enemy.

Scan the scene with me before we zoom in on effervescent Eve. She was alone in the garden. With intellect, innocence, and integrity intact, she was approached by a speaking animal. He asked about the one prohibition in God's plan for the man and woman. Because of his not-so-gentle persuasion, the woman committed an act of disobedience. It was an act to which she was not intellectually committed, but probably one to which she was moved by emotion. The consequence led to an indictment not only of herself and her husband, but of the entire human race.

After centuries of reflection, we as descendants of this hapless pair still stand aghast. How could it have happened, we are still asking; yet we know it did because we ourselves are doing the same things every day.

Theologians may put original sin into perspective with philosophical finesse, but my female nature wants to climb into Eve's thinking. It's not just curiosity; there's a key in there, a secret combination that will unlock my own stubborn savagery—that same puzzle of nature Paul described: "the good that I wish, I do not do; but I practice the very evil that I do not wish" (Rom. 7:19).

Eve's Blind Spots

I think there are at least two reasons why Eve should have concluded from the serpent's bizarre behavior, "Something isn't right!"

First, the serpent had no business talking. He was by definition a beast of the field. All plant and animal life had been created to glorify God in their particular spheres (Psalm 19) and Adam had been put in charge to subdue them. His naming process was symbolic; that is, names indicated characteristics. He had to know biology to choose names. In this harmonious, obedient creation, a talking animal was out of place. Eve knew that. This was the first signal that something was evil in Eden.

Most important and obvious is the content of what the tempter said. His initial question was a challenge to the authority and integrity of the Creator. "Did God *really* say that you should not eat of every (that is, from any) tree of the garden?" How cleverly the query is worded. The serpent (whose identity is not yet uncovered) knew quite well what God had said. He also knew that Eve knew what God had said. But knowledge must be skillfully employed; then it becomes wisdom. Eve knew the right facts and the serpent seemed to understand how easily her thinking could be short-circuited. He assumed a similar thinking posture with her.

Actually, it's an old salesman's trick, posed to create doubt. "Are you really totally satisfied with the encylopedia you now have?" Naturally, my encyclopedia is not perfect in every respect, and so I am tempted to say, "Well, no, not totally." And that admission of something less than total satisfaction opens the door for further persuasion.

In order to be honest, Eve had to explain there was one tree that was forbidden. Aha! An exception! Enough of an opening for the apparently curious inquirer to press his point. It intrigues me to observe that Eve misquoted God: "God has said, 'You shall not eat from it or touch it, lest you die.' "

Actually, God had not said anything about touching it. Was this Eve's interpretation? Not a bad one. Stay away. Don't flirt with trouble.

Another small mystery piques my thinking. This is a reference to a relationship that neither Adam nor Eve had known. She mentioned death, which was out of the range of her experience. Apparently God had given them understanding beyond their immediate world. We do not have to experience something to understand it.

Words always rest on the virtue of the speaker. Talk is cheap, unless a man is as good as his word. As for God, He cannot lie (2 Cor. 1:18). ". . . What he had promised, He was able also to perform" (Rom. 4:21). "My counsel shall stand" (Isa. 46:10, KJV). These are the words of Paul and of Isaiah. The psalmist sums it up, "Forever, O Lord, Thy word is settled in heaven" (119:89).

Then why did Eve and the serpent pursue the possibility that God did not mean what He said? Because the serpent was speaking in the framework of Satan, who was a liar from the beginning, according to the words of Jesus in John 8:44.

Dr. C. I. Scofield explains:

> Satan . . . as prince of this world system is the real though unseen ruler of the successive world powers . . . (Isa. 14:13) The serpent in his Edenic form, is not to be thought of as a writhing reptile. That is the effect of the curse. The creature which lent itself to Satan may well have been the most beautiful as it was the most 'subtle' of creatures less than man. Traces of that beauty remain despite the curse . . . In the serpent Satan appeared as an angel of light.[5]

Freedom has fences. Did Eve not recognize that fact? Was she simply a happy, frolicsome young woman, totally delighted by her home, fully unsuspecting— and unthinking? Was the ability to converse with the animals, perhaps, a playful pastime, a newly discovered skill?

Why should the graceful serpent inquire concerning God's commandment? She did possess superior intelligence. She knew the answer. Talking with the serpent was certainly not wrong. Highly unusual, perhaps, but not disobedient. Nevertheless, the consequences of that conversation were lethal.

Eve's Descent into Darkness

The master deceiver knew better than to slap on her a harsh contradiction of divine orders. Instead, he jacked up his proposition with seemingly logical reasoning: "You surely shall not die! For God knows that in the day you eat from it your eyes will be opened, and you will be like God, knowing good and evil" (Gen. 3:4–5).

Mm-mmm! She was no dullard! She listened, considered, and with womanly instinct decided at least to take a look. Did she, perhaps, have a vague foreboding that mystified and intrigued her? Could she have felt impish and impetuous? Did she simply ignore the flashing red lights?

What the serpent said was partially true. She would know good and evil. Wow! How exciting! You can almost see her goose bumps pop up as she gets ready to take a first-time joyride. Eve did not realize she had no capacity to handle evil.

The beauty, the symmetry, the fragrance of that fruit, I believe, drew her strangely toward it. With the insistent prodding of history's most wicked double cross, she doubted . . . she denied . . . she disobeyed . . . she destroyed herself, her husband, and billions of her progeny.

Blinded by the dazzle of the moment, she failed to take the whole picture into account. She concentrated momentarily on the created product rather than its Creator. She based her actions on very superficial evidence. She did not stop to throw upon the screen of her judgment the two contrasting testimonies—"if you eat . . . you shall surely die" and "ye shall not surely die." Moreover, as a member of a team she should have consulted Adam; but she was, as are her daughters centuries removed, free to make her own decisions, free to ignore what she knew was right, free to act without really thinking—but never free to escape the consequences of disobedience.

Eve "spoke," "saw," "ate," and "gave." The New Testament comments on this episode with terse reflection: "the woman being quite deceived, fell into transgression" (1 Tim. 2:14).

I know exactly how this happened. So do you. No one of us has grown to adulthood without some experience of confronting evil—and losing. Let me illustrate the process.

Some years ago when my husband and I were very new in the pastorate, I opened my front door one morning to a smooth-tongued woman who was selling cosmetics. She did not tell me that was her mission; instead she complimented my neat appearance with particular reference to how my lipstick was artfully applied so early in the day. Obviously, therefore, I was a fine little homemaker . . . blah, blah, blah . . . ad nauseum!

Looking back, it's hard to believe I was so naive. I am inclined to think Eve had that same reflecting experience. At her suggestion, I invited the woman into my home. After all, she wanted to talk with me about "something that would be of real interest." I wanted to be a friendly pastor's wife, a cooperative citizen of the community. Nothing wrong with that! Once she was installed in my living room and had inquired about the family, she proceeded to tell me a fabulous offer was being made in her line of cosmetics. She gave me free samples, and assured me I was the perfect one for this special event.

One big problem made me restless. We were not long out of graduate school, serving at a beginner's salary, paying off debts, and supporting two very young children. As man and wife, we had agreed that not an extra penny should be spent unless we both were convinced it was necessary. The moment of truth came when I had to say, "I just can't afford it."

"Oh, that's no problem! Is that what's worrying you?" she asked. "All you have to do is give me a little pocket change to hold this for you. . . ." She carefully avoided quoting the total cost, but cleverly mentioned only part of the purchase, intending to confuse me. I protested, but felt I was in too deep. I had already taken much of her time and her free samples, but I really did not have any money. I honestly did not.

"Oh, c'mon," she said, with a lighthearted laugh. "You've at least got a piggy bank for the kids!" Preposterous! But of course, that was true. Desperate now to get rid of her, I actually went back to my sleeping child's bedroom and opened the piggy bank. Of course, I apologized for the small change!

A week or so later, the fateful knock came at the door late one evening. A package was being delivered with an enormous (for us) amount due on it. I quickly paid for it out of my grocery money and tried to return to the kitchen as if nothing had happened. Husbands, however, have a way of asking, "Who was that?" Eventually the whole story had to be told—and told it was with tears and penitence and promise of atonement. But the dastardly deed had been done, and nothing could undo it. Nothing could wipe away the consequences, the disappointment, the breach of faith, the horrible embarrassment and humiliation. "Oh, honey, not *you!*" Yes, me. I know something of Eve's dilemma because I am made from the same bolt of cloth.

Adam's Complicity

Adam may have feared separation, I think, from his beloved beauty. The New Testament informs us that Adam was not deceived (or at least not totally—1 Tim. 2:14). His free will was also exercised to disobedience. By himself he probably would never have given the serpent the time of day; that's why the serpent went to Eve. But Adam did not love the serpent as he loved Eve.

Every loved wife knows she has hidden power to bend her husband's will in her direction. When *Eve* offered the forbidden fruit, Adam ate it.

Facing the Creator

Can you possibly imagine the dread of listening for the voice of God? Adam and Eve had often reveled in His voice, but now it was different. They had a guilty conscience. Little wonder that Adam says, "I heard the sound of thee in the garden, and I was afraid. . . ."

He was afraid not because God is by nature angry and vindictive. It was not the fear of the prisoner for the harsh jailer, but the debilitating guilt of one who has defaulted in the face of beauty, freedom, love, and generosity.

"Where are you?" Adam used his nakedness to defend his disappearance. How absurd! God had created him unclothed. Ever since I have been a little girl, sensitive about being seen without clothes, I have wondered about this matter of nakedness which popped up so early in history.

Today, nudity is flaunted as a saucy rebellion against the square establishment. As a very practical issue, I am confronted as a woman—and as a mother of daughters—with how much undressing is too much. The frightening part is that the standards change, and so do I. What I may have considered immodest ten years ago is now perfectly normal and acceptable.

God explained very carefully before the serpent ever danced onto the stage that "the man and his wife were both naked and were not ashamed" (Gen. 2:25). Then, immediately after Adam and Eve had eaten the forbidden fruit, "the eyes of both of them were opened, and they knew that they were naked. . . ."

Dr. Edward J. Young comments:

> It is not of the physical eyes that the Scripture speaks here, when it states that their eyes were "opened" for Adam and Eve had not been physically blind. . . . Rather the reference is to the arousing of the conscience and an awakening of the understanding so that the man and the woman now see themselves in a tragic condition and seek deliverance therefrom.[6]

Spiritual death had already started to deteriorate the now-sinful couple. Shame and guilt are part of that death status. Is the instinctive need to cover our bodies a merciful visual aid of the need for covering our guilt? I think so. Does it follow, then, that the ability to ignore that self-consciousness is a healthy victory? Obviously not. God Himself provided the first wardrobe from animal skins. Noah sinned when in his drunken stupor after the flood his nakedness was uncovered.

Read about the Israelites just after God had given Moses the Law on Mount Sinai. Moses returned to find them, under Aaron's leadership, worshiping a golden calf, and the record says . . . "Moses saw that the people were naked; (for Aaron had made them naked unto their shame among their enemies)" (Ex. 32:25, KJV). To purge this sin from the camp, the Levites were commanded to kill the offenders, and three thousand men died.

Nakedness in the Scriptures is often related to poverty and shame. Christ's words, "I was . . . naked and you clothed me. . . ." illustrates that He regards lack of clothing as a sign of humiliation. Paul speaks of being clothed in the righteousness of Christ. Job reminds us that "naked I came from my mother's womb, and naked I shall return there." God sees us as we are, but gives us the promise that not even nakedness shall separate us from the love of God (Rom. 8:35).

I still need discretion in my day-to-day dressing. There are guidelines. Modesty is the standard (1 Peter

3), but the standards vary. Fortunately, God has given us common sense, as well as the Holy Spirit who promises to lead us into all truth. I can know what's right for me. He gives me—not the current issue of *Vogue*—but a sense of propriety.

Don't Blame Me!

God refused to allow His interrogation to be detoured. He moved right to the issue at hand. "Have you eaten from the tree of which I commanded you not to eat?" (Gen. 3:11). God gave a reminder, a re-statement of the command!

Here was Adam's first opportunity to tell the truth, to ask for forgiveness. Instead he gave an excuse. In the showdown before the Almighty, Adam blamed his wife for his actions. You can almost see the beads of perspiration of Adam's brow as he fidgets and points a finger at Eve. "The woman whom thou gavest . . ." He put the blame indirectly on God—it's all really because of what You did, God. You really cannot blame me. It was her idea—and she was your idea—and I just went along with her.

In a sense it was true; but no, he—the leader—was responsible and it was on him that God placed primary blame. God first asked Adam to name his sin. His weak, pass-the-buck reply did not even merit a divine answer. God then quizzed Eve, culpable, responsible for her own actions. She pointed her finger at the serpent.

Parents often witness this kind of lame reasoning with children. Sister comes home dragging dirty little brother. Questioning ends up with "I couldn't help it—he wanted to walk on the curb, and the car came. . . ."

Since Adam and Eve are our ancestors and, as well,

co-defendants before the bar of God's justice, we try to vindicate them. There is much circumstantial evidence that ought to be heard, we say. Couldn't God overlook a little first offense? It's really just a kind of Jack and Jill: "Eve fell down and broke her crown and Adam came tumbling after." So, why can't you just pick yourself up and promise to be more careful next time?

The problem is there's a war on. A spiritual conflict. The serpent was simply a front for the real villain. Something happened back before Eden. Isaiah opens the attic closet and shows us a skeleton. (Isaiah 14) Lucifer said to God "I will be like the most High. . . ." and sin began. Eve was simply the first human victim. Satan had declared eternal war against God, and this was the first recorded skirmish on earth. That explains why God wrote the bottom line in bold black ink. We call it *the curse*.

(To the serpent [Satan]:)
Because you have done this, cursed are you more than all cattle, and more than every beast of the field; on your belly shall you go, and dust shall you eat all the days of your life; and I will put enmity between you and the woman, and between your seed and her seed; he shall bruise you on the head, and you shall bruise him on the heel.

(To the woman:)
I will greatly multiply your pain in childbirth, in pain you shall bring forth children; yet your desire shall be for your husband, and he shall rule over you.

(To Adam:)
Because you have listened to the voice of your wife, and have eaten from the tree about which I have commanded you, saying, "You shall not eat from it"; cursed is the ground because of you; in toil you shall eat of it all the days of your life. Both thorns and thistles it shall grow for

you; and you shall eat the plants of the field; by the sweat
of your face you shall eat bread, till you return to the
ground, because from it you were taken; for you are dust,
and to dust you shall return. (Gen. 3:14–19)

These words closed that chapter in Eden. The honeymoon was over. Adam and Eve were like a house
damaged in a storm. The parts of the structure were
there, but they were dying and in disarray. Their innocence was gone. They had exercised their free will to
disobey their Creator. God relocated Adam and Eve—
outside the garden, away from the tree of life. There
they would begin the harsh, uphill battle adjusting to a
life independent from God.

Phase III–The High Cost of Living Outside Eden

Night of Terror
Some years ago I spent my silver wedding anniversary in the Swiss Alps. I wanted very much to see the
beautiful, snow-covered peak of the Matterhorn, but it
was covered by clouds and people in the mountain
towns told us it was rarely visible. Then one day we
watched as the clouds moved rapidly and the sun
burned through, first in patches, then in large, clear
spots. And there—for just a brief moment—we saw it!
Etched in pristine glory against a blue sky, the peak
looked like a monstrous, hooded giant sitting on the
earth. Glorious but awesome.

Much of history is hidden in the dark clouds of despair, oppression, suffering, and failure. But for Eve,
the third phase of her life began with the clean air of
exhilaration.

Good morning, world! Guess what? There is a lilt of
triumph in Eve's greeting as she cries out in the first
verse of Genesis 4, "I have gotten a manchild with the

help of the Lord." A tiny, helpless manchild. The only other person in the world was a man—her brilliant, gifted partner-husband. Now there was another and her heart sang out loud. Her song reverberates through the centuries. Many of us have shared the shining moment of her joy. The hope of a bright future comes at that first sight of the newborn child, so exquisitely formed, utterly tender and innocent, and he is *mine*. A little Adam. Never, perhaps, was a child born with higher hopes and warmer reception. God Himself had given the command to be fruitful and multiply and replenish the earth. This child marked the first step. And little Cain followed his father in learning the pursuit of agriculture.

Again another son—Abel. Joy, exultation, thanksgiving. Love poured out to these sons. The record does not satisfy our curiosity about the human factors that added up to produce the first family explosion. We must make certain deductions as we look at the murder, the sibling rivalry.

Parenthood was then, as it is now, a precarious profession. Balancing indulgence with limitation is a feat that requires supernatural wisdom. Love can sometimes blur our vision. Was Cain, like Jacob, a "mama's boy" who got his own way, or had too much too soon? Or was Adam so resentful about being evicted from the Garden that he was too rigid and harsh, so that Cain rebelled? I personally wonder whether Eve knew what the Lord God meant when He told her, ". . . in pain you shall bring forth children. . . ."

Recap her career. She had been created in the midst of a mysterious hush, wherein God took Adam's rib and handcrafted her body. There was no quotation from Eve, but the meeting of the two sent Adam into personal philosophic rapture. We would say, colloquially, she blew his mind.

But one seemingly small decision converted paradise into prison. Having been released by a God of grace, these fledgling pioneers, wearing their coats of skin, set about tilling the cursed ground.

God was not "mad" at them; He was merciful. Even though His holiness and justice demanded that Adam and Eve lived with the consequences of their disobedience, God provided clothing and instilled in them abilities (prior training) to survive in an alien world.

Small wonder, then, that after many difficult days, Eve's joy was boundless when her first son was born. If today the birth of a healthy child is cause for rejoicing, how much more in that lonely barrenness where she and her husband farmed for a living. Eve saw God's hand in her life. She knew the source of this precious little baby was God Himself. Little did she realize that Adam's seed, implanted in that new life, was a time bomb of personal disaster.

And then there were two! The second child of the same sex seems to come into the world with less fanfare. But he is still very important, especially in this first family. With God and his people, names were always suggestive—both of the purpose for the life and often as a prophecy.

Cain was first; his name meant "acquisition." Abel means "that which ascends." The first seems to be pulling everything down to himself, while the other is sending everything up. They were indeed opposites. Very little background is available, but we cannot escape the black headlines of fratricide.

"Cain rose up against Abel his brother and killed him" (Gen. 4:8). How can that be? We knock on the door of our friend Eve to ask some questions. It's incredible.

Eve's spirit is devastated. Her rousing announcement that the Adam family had expanded to three, then four, has been deflated. The divine words, spoken in the heat of her embarrassment after the serpent episode, had dulled somewhat. But now they are pulsing like a raging fever in her brain: ". . . in pain you shall bring forth children. . . ." Pain. So *this* was part of the price tag. That fresh grave—that peculiar ache of a son wandering—you do not know where. . . .

I suspect that a thousand questions anchored that first beautiful woman to an emotional valley. Had she overindulged that first son? Had Adam failed in his teaching responsibility? Why hadn't she sensed the incompatibility and somehow intervened? Was Cain, after all, more like his mother? Why did she listen to that serpent and ruin everything? Tragedy is hard enough to sustain by yourself, but having to watch your child go through it is indescribable agony.

Dr. Roy Zuck, in a gripping saga of his daughter's injury and recovery from a near-fatal auto accident, expressed vividly his own feelings in a chapter entitled "The Long Saturday." "Like giant rats, those questions began to gnaw at my mind. But I kept them to myself, not wanting to add to Dottie's fear. And yet I realized she was probably thinking similar questions."[7]

Shock, grief, exhaustion, and then inevitably the slow painful process of analysis. What are the cold facts, in the light of a new day?

It all centered on this sacrifice situation. God had slain animals and used the skins for clothing. Instructions had obviously been given; the symbolic death of the animals atoned for offenses against God's Holy Person—in prospect of a perfect Person who was to come and die for the sin of man.

Sacrifice is bloody. Who wants to kill a lovable, healthy little lamb who never hurt anything? But God had commanded it. It was a matter of obedience to authority. Not *that* again! Yes, it's the same song, second verse.

Review the conversation between Cain and God. Big brother was going around with a frown on his face. He was downright put out with God about this offering thing. After all, if a man has prize orchards and grain fields, what's wrong with bringing a sample of his best specimens? It's not like he was ignoring God.

"Why are you angry, Cain?" How could Cain tell Him, "The truth is, I'm angry with you, God. I think you're prejudiced in favor of Abel"? Jehovah obviously knew that and followed with an offer, a last chance to avert catastrophe. God understood his thinking. Simply humble yourself and make the proper offering; "Without shedding of blood there is no forgiveness" (Heb. 9:22). After that, you will still be the elder brother, ruler of the house.

No! Premeditated murder! Cain's pride was outraged and he headed straight for his brother. We cannot know what happened except that "Cain rose up against Abel his brother and killed him."

His motive is given many years later by John (1 John 3:12)." Not as Cain, who was of the evil one, and slew his brother. And for what reason did he slay him? Because his deeds were evil, and his brother's were righteous." You can almost hear Satan chuckling as he wins round two. Cain, like his father and mother, yielded to a tragic attachment to the creation, rather than to the Creator.

Did Eve ever know what happened to Cain? Possibly. In any event she had lost both of her sons. Yet we see God remained faithful to Eve in her loss, for when her third son, Seth, came into the world, she again gives God the credit: "God . . . has appointed me another offspring in place of Abel, for Cain killed him" (Gen. 4:25).

It was her grandson Enosh, Seth's boy, who finally got it together with God. "And to Seth, to him also a son was born; and he called his name Enosh. Then men began to call upon the name of the Lord" (Gen. 4:26).

Lessons from Eve

Hilltops of joy and valleys of sorrow; Eve ran the gamut of emotions. She is the prototype of every normal little girl born on earth. God's purpose for her is the highest imaginable. Her own fallen impulses are her enemies.

The text of Genesis dresses our first mother in a complete garb. She was secure in her identity, certain of her function, and free to pursue unlimited challenges. No mooring lines held her. The dangerous part about free will is that every time we exercise it, good judgment must prevail. And good judgment really needs supernatural oversight. God had created her in His own image, but she certainly did not have God's all-knowing mind.

Did this, then, put Eve on a slippery deck with no guardrail? Not really. She had a command, a "do not" from God. That was her main protection. But she also had a husband with a will to care for her. He was many things to her—lover, companion, co-respondent in every activity. And she needed him just as he needed her. Making a major decision without his input was fatal.

When a woman has a husband who clearly and unmistakably loves and adores her, she is more relaxed, less cautious, but more apt to overstep boundaries, and prone to forget her function. I don't know why, but I know it's the way we women are.

Why did God in the curse arrange to have her husband rule over her? Any law bears the mark of the law-giver. This very early glimpse into God's character shows Him to be just, righteous, and protective of His creation. We mortals invariably look at law as prohibition. For example, "Thou shalt not commit adultery." That is prohibition, we insist. But is it? Does this command not also imply God wishes His people to be kept *from* something, and also—most importantly—*for* something? A sexual purity of life guards the home, the children, the very future of the race.

Sometimes we women look at it from the inside out—we interpret headship as hardship or imprisonment. Make no mistake: an ungodly man can be a real hardship. It is only as we accept our position in Christ that the benefits of that relationship are ours.

A beautiful thoroughbred mare in heat, for example, may be kept penned up—not because the owner hates her or is trying to punish her, but to protect her from the stallions who would defile her. Sure she has spirit and capability and is in every way equal to her male counterpart; perhaps she could even beat him in a race. Her very potential makes her a prize to be sheltered. Our heavenly Owner knows what is best for women in the long run. Why do we persist in trying to kick the slats out of our protection?

Elisabeth Elliot says it perfectly:

> If you can understand your womanhood . . . you will know the fullness of life. Hear the call of God to be a woman. Obey that call. Turn your energies to service. Whether your service is to be to a husband and through him and the family and home God gives you to serve the

world, or whether you should remain, in the providence of God, single in order to serve the world without the solace of husband, home, and family, you will know fullness of life, fullness of liberty, and (I know whereof I speak) fullness of joy.[8]

Study Questions: Chapter 1

Eve was created to live in beauty and fulfillment with her husband and her Maker. She is remembered chiefly because she flaunted her independence and free will, thus introducing sin into the human race.

1. Discuss the disobedience of Adam and Eve in the light of this quotation from the British Journal of Criminology:

   Psychological studies advise that attitudes change to fit behavior more than vice versa, so it's easy to justify something you've already done. . . . If you just do it, it's not so bad. You don't have time to feel guilty. The socialization process is rapid. . . .*

2. Romans 5 refers back to the Garden of Eden:

   "As by one man sin entered the world . . . (v. 12)
   ". . . death reigned from Adam to Moses . . . (v. 14)
   ". . . by the transgression of the one the many died . . ." (v. 15)
   "by the transgression of the one, death reigned . . ." (v. 17)
   "through one man's disobedience   ." (v. 19)

What is the force of "one man" when the record actually states that Eve disobeyed first?

*Vol. 15, No. 3, Albert Velarde, University of Washington, reported by Gary Gregg in *Psychology Today*, September 1976.

2

Sarah: Brains, Beauty, and Bedlam

Her name was Gayla, but it did not fit her face nor her stooped-shouldered dejection. The divorce had become final three weeks ago. She had not slept since then, except for gnawed-off fits of exhaustion. Why was she here, at a conference on marriage?

"I don't really know why I'm here. After all, it's too late for me, I guess—isn't it?"

She looked at me with eyes that pleaded for understanding and a kind of desparate SOS for help.

"I'm going to school now," she said, as if this tidbit would feed my support for her. "I'm over-qualified, they say, and so I'm learning to type."

This tall, once-confident woman had a master's degree in chemistry, but in the midst of professional success her twenty-year-old marriage had exploded in her face. Her career had disintegrated with her home. The shattered pieces she picked up verbally to explain to me were all too familiar, fitting into a pattern of pain I've heard over and over again as I've talked with women of my world in many places.

I wanted to cry as I listened and tried to imagine what

it would be like if my own children were to testify against me in a court of law, as hers had done. But sympathy would not change things.

I wanted to hug her and say "It's gonna be all right" when she described her loneliness because of a husband who had "checked out." But my encouragement could not fill her void.

I wanted to spank her like a child when she related her own selfish, rude remarks which had alienated her family. But there could be no help in scolding!

The only healing balm I could give her was God's promise: "My grace is sufficient for you, for power is perfected in weakness" (2 Cor. 12:9).

Up to the breaking point of her marriage, Gayla would not shed her pride to admit her weaknesses. Now confidence had been stripped from her for all the world to see; she was searching for some miracle to cover the shame.

Gayla typifies thousands of modern women concentrating on a career, assuming the family will take care of itself—a gross miscalculation. She believed in herself; why didn't her husband and children believe in her? And when it all fell apart, she still wanted to blame her husband—and the institution of marriage. She was utterly confused and disillusioned.

We married women are in danger of being sold into a slavery of self. Marriage is not only workable; it is one of the highest forms of human fulfillment. But we must play by God's rules or we will lose every time.

Measuring Marriage by God's Yardstick

God the Creator made marriage in an orderly fashion and blessed it. The exciting part is He is still blessing it today. The world may have gone mad and be swirling around in disarray, but I can have a serene center of gravity, another flesh-and-blood person very close to me who cares, who shares, who loves. Geographical distance is not important because commitment is there and we both count on it. Our relationship is alive and pulsating, healthy and mutually rewarding.

It does not just happen. For me it is the product of more than thirty years' work. I could detail for you the first faltering steps, those early days when I thought I was sure I didn't want him—for a husband, that is. Then I wasn't sure. Then I began to be sure I did. I could describe my family's ambivalence about marriage to someone from a broken home, and why they had reason to be worried.

But my story would be just that—a story. You could say: well, that's how it went for you. That's nice. Thank you. Goodbye.

Instead, I have a story you *must* hear because God wrote it. When He talks, we'd all better listen. He tucked this mini-marriage manual into the first book of the Bible, but it has pollinated millions of people since then. Sarah, wife of Abraham, is my heroine.

She is singled out in two instances in the New Testament for special commendation. Those two medals of honor form the key, I believe, to unlocking the secret of successful marriage.

The first citation: *she obeyed her husband.*

In the same way, you wives, be submissive to your own husbands so that even if any of them are disobedient to the word, they may be won without a word by the behavior of their wives, as they observe your chaste and respectful behavior. And let not your adornment be external only—braiding the hair, and wearing gold jewelry, and putting on dresses; but let it be the hidden person of the heart, with the imperishable quality of a gentle and quiet spirit, which is precious in the sight of God. For in this way in former times the holy women also, who hoped in God, used to adorn themselves, being submissive to their own husbands. Thus Sarah obeyed Abraham, calling him lord, and you have become her children if you do what is right without being frightened by any fear (1 Pet. 3:1–6).

The second citation: *she believed what God had promised.*

By faith even Sarah herself received ability to conceive, even beyond the proper time of life, since she considered Him faithful who had promised (Heb. 11:11).

Family on the Move

Early in Genesis, the family of Shem, Noah's oldest son, narrowed to a thread in the person of Terah. Three sons were born of this man; the first, named Abram, married his half-sister and lived in the city of Ur. In our frame of reference, this occurred in the Bronze Age in the locality of the Fertile Crescent.

(Ur) was a leading Sumerian city, possessed an elaborate system of writing, advanced means of mathematical, astronomical and astrological computation, a mature and comprehensive religious organization, highly developed business and commercial procedures, a form of art, a flourishing educational system, and other marks of a cultured society.[2]

From this city the family migrated hundreds of miles northwesterly along the Euphrates River. At Terah's death, God appeared to Abram and issued traveling orders, destination unknown.

With the ease and simplicity modern life affords, homemakers are still notoriously negative about moving. How much more must Sarai have dreaded the prospect of becoming a nomad, living on a permanent campout. But she was wise, knowing that if there had to be a choice, a good relationship with her husband was far more important than a comfortable home. Her seventy-five-year-old spouse had received God's direction and His promise of blessing. Together they moved with all their cattle, servants, and goods. They had only their faith in Jehovah to lead the way.

The Inside Story on Sarah

Until God changed her name to Sarah at age ninety, Abram's wife was known as Sarai. She enjoyed two assets: wealth and beauty. Besides being the wife of a shrewd herdsman and administrator, she was also strikingly fair, a fact which occasioned her panic-stricken husband to lie twice to kings about his relationship to her. She was greatly respected and loved by her husband, an enviable position for any wife.

One persistent problem clouded her life. It drops with a thud on the reader: "Sarai was barren; she had no child" (Gen. 11:30). In our overpopulated world this curse can hardly be appreciated; yet in Abram's day its sad implications can hardly be emphasized enough. Still, Abram never voluntarily took another wife while Sarah lived.

Sarai faithfully followed the long, circuitous life of her patriarch husband, surely with many distressful moments.

Consider the flight to Egypt, when Abram's faith was not strong enough to trust God for survival in famine-stricken Canaan. There Sarah willingly conspired with him to pose as his sister in order to save his life.

Such deception was humanly logical. The Pharaoh was certainly not above killing a man to gain his beauti-

ful wife for the harem. That was common oriental practice. But Abram and Sarai had not been directed by
God to go to Egypt, and so it was with an inner tension
that they presented themselves to the monarch and lied
to him.

Together they made the pact to deceive. Their faith
was still a slender thread. It is only after trials and
triumphs that faith grows and toughens in us weak
humans. And once a sin is committed, how easy it is to
do it again. Years later, Abraham and Sarah again re-
verted to their old behavior when a similar instance
arose.

Horrified at the fiery downfall of Sodom, they fled
the scene and were again faced by a powerful king,
Abimilech. What else could they do but drag out the
secondhand fraud? Sarah had rehearsed that scene; she
knew the lines. "And she, even herself said, 'He is my
brother' . . ." (Gen. 20:5). They risked Sarah's chastity
and the purity of the promised seed. They dishonored
God because Abraham was well-known as Jehovah's
servant. Even the seasoned man of faith is always subject to weakness and temptation.

Sarah's Plan to Solve God's Problem

During the stay in Egypt, Sarai acquired a hand-
maiden named Hagar. She had taken the girl away
from her family and the Egyptian civilization to go to
an unsettled land. Hagar's family was obviously poor
and Sarai was a favorite in Pharaoh's palace. Who
would say her nay? Hagar left her home, probably
willingly, and became the personal slave of the beautiful Sarai.

Dr. Alexander Whyte of Scotland has written:

As time went on, and as the hope of any possibility of her

ever becoming a mother died out in Sarah's heart, humility, and resignation, and the blotting-out of herself had but grown apace with her disappointment, that would have hid Sarah from all her temptations . . . but her terrible cross had but inflamed her to find some wild and willful way for herself to live any longer such an embarrassment to her husband, such an evident obstacle to the prosperity of his house, and such an eye-sore and jest to all the camp and to all the country around.[3]

Time, distance, and discouragement uncovered Sarai's feline qualities. With the soft pad of her paw she motioned Hagar to take her place, to have a baby, to solve God's problem. How utterly foolish to think we can tell God how to do it! Then, caught in the net of her own design, frustrated by Hagar's insolence, Sarah dealt out harsh punishment and her slave ran away.

Sarai bared her claws. The gentle, beautiful Sarai turned beast! We have no cause to criticize. Is there one of us who has not hurt an innocent person to save our own reputation and to cover our own stupid mistakes?

God's gentle dealing with Hagar is a salve for every disillusioned girl who has been used and misused by our own insensitive society. How many are caught in the glitter of the rich and the powerful, only to be made their slaves, only to be pitilessly thrown out when they become weights?

An angel confronted Hagar (Genesis 16) with two questions to bring her to her senses: Where did you come from? Where are you going? She truthfully answered: "I am fleeing from the presence of my mistress Sarai." She knew no answer to the second question. "Return to your mistress, and submit yourself to her authority," the angel commanded. Never does God condone insubordination. With the rebuke came a promise. Her son would be called Ishmael, father of a great nation, a wild and warlike man.

With Ishmael's birth Abram began to see this boy as his heir of the promise, but he had not yet learned that God means *exactly* what He says. Four years later, when Abram was ninety-nine years old, God came again to confirm His promise and to change his name. No longer would he be Abram, but Abraham; not just "exalted father," but "father of a multitude."

Likewise, Sarai was to become Sarah, literally "princess." God was giving birth to a new nation and He was proclaiming royal status for its progenitors. Sarah, He promised, would bear a son.

"Then Abraham fell on his face and laughed, and said in his heart, 'Will a child be born to a man one hundred years old? And will Sarah, who is ninety years old, bear a child?' " (Gen. 17:17).

Incredible! But again God repeated the promise and gave to Abraham the name for his son, Isaac.

God Makes Good His Promise

Not long after that, Abraham spotted three men approaching his tent at midday. With characteristic hospitality he ran to welcome them, washed their feet, and offered refreshment. As was the custom, the men ate together while Sarah stood apart behind the tent door.

"Where is Sarah?" they asked.

"In the tent," answered the host.

"I will certainly return to you at this time next year, and Sarah your wife shall have a son."

Now it was Sarah's turn to laugh. Not aloud, but within herself. But the angel heard. "Why did Sarah laugh? Is anything too difficult for the Lord? . . . . Sarah shall have a son."

Having announced impending birth, the angels departed toward Sodom to announce impending death. Sarah, embarrassed for laughing and caught again lying, must have taken giant strides in her process of believing God. Perhaps that question rang over and over again in her mind: Is anything too difficult for the Lord?

Sarah's life had been a series of supernatural deliverances, of divine victories, of demonstrations of God's power in the midst of idolatrous and wicked people. Undoubtedly, the ghastly demise of Sodom had terrified her. Then at Gerar she witnessed the amazing disentanglement from the clutches of Abimelech. She was finally convinced God could do it. She would not deny His word. She had to believe; there was no other solution to the problem. If God did not miraculously provide the baby, there would be no child. She believed the impossible for herself and God honored her faith. It took ninety years of preparation.

Unprecedented rejoicing came to the tent of Abraham with the birth of Isaac. Any birth would have caused joy, but this miracle was a special proof of God's reliability. When Isaac was weaned at the age of three, Abraham made a great feast. Never before had the family known such a celebration.

Watching from the wings with narrowed eyes were Ishmael and his mother, Hagar. Again there was rudeness, mocking, jealousy. Again Sarah reacted with anger; she asked Abraham to cast them both out.

The tender nature of Abraham recoiled at the thought of such severe treatment. He had come to love his son Ishmael. Yet God Himself affirmed Sarah's judgment. ". . . listen to her, for through Isaac your descendants shall be named" (Gen. 21:12).

Once again Hagar was alone in the wilderness and once more in her hour of extremity she was confronted by the voice of God. "What is the matter with you, Hagar? Do not fear . . ." (Gen. 21:17). Miraculously He provided water and sustenance for both Hagar and

Ishmael. Life went on, and the record notes that Hagar procured for her son a wife from Egypt. She took him back home to meet the family.

Sarah lived to be 127 years old. Her death and burial are uniquely recorded, the only woman so immortalized in the Scriptures. We can readily see why God weaves this woman into the exquisite tapestries of the New Testament. She was married to a man with a rare aptitude for believing God and she learned from him, I believe, the secret of faith. She learned first through obedience. Peter says she called him "lord"; that is, she held her husband in high respect and bowed to his wishes.

What must it have been like to be uprooted from a comfortable city home to a tent in desolate, undeveloped country? Abraham apparently kept talking about a future city of great beauty and spiritual stability. Periodically in his quest for it, he gathered his family and offered animal sacrifices upon stone altars to teach them about the nature of God. Jehovah periodically conversed with Abraham, giving him instructions, making unbelievable promises, and blessing him with an abundance of worldly goods.

Sarah watched—and learned. In her own private disillusionment and anguish she finally decided, Jehovah God is trustworthy. Against all human logic, God was going to give her a son. She believed, for no other reason than God said so. "She considered Him faithful who had promised (Heb. 11:11)." God holds her up and says to every woman who reads the Bible, "This is how it's done. Just do what I tell you and believe what I say."

The models of faith who are displayed by God in the eleventh chapter of Hebrews include only this one wife. She is enthroned in the elect company of those whom God says continue to speak throughout history.

Sarah's decision to believe God related to a very human matter. She was simply too aged, physically, to bear a child; nevertheless, the Scriptures report she received strength by herself and delivered the child. The original language uses the adverb "even." "Through faith even Sarah herself received strength . . ." (Heb. 11:11, KJV). It is a clue that the whole matter was highly unnatural. It is also an arrow which sends the inquisitive reader back to find out why. How did Sarah leap from the ranks of the many godly women of ancient Israel to the place of honor beside her husband in the book of Hebrews?

Sarah: Her Husband and Her God

The answer to that question may sound quaint to modern ears, but the plain fact is that she was submissive to her husband (1 Pet. 3:6). In that attitude of obedience and subjection she learned the priceless lesson of faith. In the end she got it together spiritually, but she started out merely being an obedient wife.

One evening one of my young adult children thoughtlessly placed a wet glass on a lamp table in the den and left it there overnight. I was appalled and dismayed the next day when I found it and saw the ugly, water stain on the warped wooden finish.

"Why," I asked myself, "cannot these kids realize the beauty of a piece of furniture like this? Why don't they think?"

I am sure this is just a small picture of what God must feel about the way we treat the delicate and exquisite relationship of marriage. We fail to see the flawless beauty of His divine intentions. We carelessly stain our marriage relationship with no thought of the damage we are causing.

Submission

It has been wisely said that "submission is the life-style of the Christian" (Eph. 5:21; 1 Pet. 2:13, etc.). But I want to talk specifically about wives submitting to husbands. The very mention of the term is like waving a red flag. Why? Because submission has been greatly misunderstood and widely misapplied.

But it's there—in 1 Peter 3, in Ephesians 5, in Colossians 3, in Titus 2, and strongly implied in 1 Corinthians 11, 1 Timothy 2, and elsewhere. The word in Greek is *hupotasso,* originally a military term meaning "to rank under." Let's not water it down—that's what it means.

Peter's words "You wives, be submissive to your own husbands" was written to dispersed Jewish believers in Christ. They were suffering persecution and Peter was writing to help them live successfully in the midst of it. And so he says, make this one mark distinctive of your lifestyle and you will see some radical changes.

Why wives? Because it was unexpected and not commonly practiced in those days any more than in our own. Since the husband-wife relationship is the core unit of society, if you put that in forward gear you've got things moving. Furthermore, it's contagious. When the wife obeys the husband, the children obey the parents. Respect for authority prevails.

"Be submissive" is a verb in the imperative mood, present tense, middle voice. That is, here is a command, to be practiced with continuous action, and with reflexive force—you do it to yourself.

Important! Nowhere in the Bible is the husband told to make the wife submit. It is *always* a voluntary submission. And it is always balanced with a command to the husband to love the wife. There are no qualifications; that is, submit only if you are loved, or love only if you are submitted to. This is a straightforward charge: be submissive. It is always to be an act of my will.

I see a difference between obedience and submission. For example, my clock wakes me in the morning. I *obey* and I get up. I cannot honestly say I *submit*. I often have an unwilling spirit! At night, that same clock tells me when to go to bed—and I gladly *submit*.

God's plan for marriage is mutual submission. Both submit to each other, but he is to submit with love; she is to submit by willingly placing him as her leader. Having said this, I have only to glance in my thick files to realize that more is being written to counter this viewpoint of submission than to support it.

Listen to the opening words of a book edited by two eminent sociologists:

There is little question that alternate life styles such as multilateral marriage, cluster families, permissive monogamy, mate-swapping, and homosexual marriage are here to stay. Further, it is becoming increasingly clear that alternate life styles and marital-familiar patterns need to be openly recognized as both legally and socially desirable for those who, for whatever reason, choose them. (The traditional must be changed) even though that pattern is destructive and productive of malaise, ennui, and disillusionment.[1]

Marriage Today

I am often involved with my husband in marriage seminars where the members of the audience are invited to write down the most pressing question in their marriage. As I have looked over many of these unsigned questions, the bulk of them have to do with four problem areas.

1. *Basic commitment.* If you live with the idea that you might have found a better partner, you are sure to find someone who appears (at a distance) to fit your idea of "better." Marriage is not obeying (or rescinding) a man-made law, like voting an amendment to the constitution. It is a divine creation—God instituted it. He did not command it, but rather made us to desire it. It cannot be outlawed any more than we can outlaw the rising ocean tide.

Marriage involves not so much love as *will*. The Bible does not teach that we fall in love and get married. The sociologist Rollo May has written, "the opposite of love is not hate, but apathy [a withdrawal of feeling], a statement that they don't matter, a suspension of commitment."[4] The opposite of will, he says, quoting William James, is being uninvolved, unrelated to significant events.

2. *Total dedication.* This dimension adds honor and respect to commitment, and calls forth personal responsibility. Live each day as if it were the last. When we give it all we've got (as we do in the honeymoon or in a crisis), we will not stagnate. The winner makes a lifestyle out of total effort.

As a wife, you are a moving object—what direction are you going—toward him or away from him? Your purpose is to be a helpmeet, the missing piece of his puzzle, the one he cannot live without.

Dedication involves *knowing* your man. Make him be able to say "She understands me." Everything in your life should be related to him; some indirectly, but all connected.

Many people are both committed and dedicated. But marriage needs more. . . .

3. *The joy of living.* Fun people are magnetic. They have forgiven the past and are full of zest for the present and hope for the future.

We are often guilty of deceptive advertising in marriage. Many of us never show outwardly the real satisfaction that loving produces. Joy spills over and infects others. This is why our little children who interrupt us with a big hug and kiss and "I wuv you" are irresistible.

Many people are committed, dedicated, and fun to be with, but they're just good friends. We wouldn't want them for marriage partners. Marriage has an extra dimension. . . .

4. *Intimacy.* A marriage partner is the receiver of your personal statement to the world. Private life is personal, original, and creative—you have to think it up yourself. There is depth of human encounter with emotional presence. It should be characterized by openness and a high degree of caring for each other, and practiced in a climate of trust and fidelity.

Lois Wyse has written in *Love Poems for the Very Married:*

There is within each of us a private place
For thinking private thoughts
And dreaming private dreams
But in the shared experience of marriage
Some people cannot stand the private partner.
How fortunate for me
That you have let me grow

Think my private thoughts
Dream my private dream
And bring a private me
To the shared experience of marriage.[5]

Marriage is a total relationship, at the heart of which is sexual expression. The sexual aspect should be the most fun-filled dimension of intimacy. I once saw a cartoon showing a tired, bedraggled couple on their honeymoon: "How many more happy, carefree days do we have to go?"

The sex drive is powerful, pervasive, a dynamic force in the will to relate. It colors everything else dull gray if it is poor, but it lights up the whole world when it is rich. Some people try to avoid its reality, like the woman who heard about Darwin's discoveries and commented: "Let's hope that it isn't true; and if it is, that it won't become generally known."

The sexual relationship is normal, designed by God. It completes the marriage relationship and enriches it. Lately, lots of people have strategized it and gotten tangled up with the contemporary "how-to" manuals. True, physical love should be cultivated, but aiming for a mythical performance level is foolish.

The sexual component in marriage is the ultimate opportunity to escape the dehumanizing effect of technology. But without commitment, without dedication, without the joy of living, it cannot be satisfying.

The Sine Qua Non *of Christian Marriage*

One more thing: Marriage as the Bible teaches it will never make sense unless it is seen from God's viewpoint. Eve disobeyed Him in Eden, and with the curse came the sentence of spiritual death which included the rule of the man over his wife. We may debate it, hate it, ignore it, or deny it, but it will not go away. It is a fact of history.

God has provided Himself as the solution. A husband and wife united to each other, and each vitally related to Jesus Christ, provides the invincible basis for married life. Freedom in marriage grows out of giving one's partner to God.

"I can do all things through Him who strengthens me (Phil. 4:13). That includes submitting to my husband, and believing what God says. I do it to please Him who died for me. Jesus Christ wants to be the third person in my marriage.

Recognize marriage as a gift of inestimable value. Take care of it. Make yourself easy to love. In order for a husband to be what God has designed for him, you must be what God has designed for you. If you try to run him, you'll ruin him. He will be frustrated and a frustrated man is never a good lover.

Yes, you have rights. But rights require responsibility and the freedom *not* to exercise them. It's how you use your freedom that God observes. He reported Sarah's performance record—that's a reminder He is also keeping records on me.

Study Questions: Chapter 2

1. A popular women's magazine conducted a three-
   month-long study of 384 marriages in 43 cities. Con-
   sulting 239 experts, the editors concluded: they are
   all marrying for a single reason: commitment.*
   Sarah also married for commitment. What is the
   difference, if any, between her marriage and the
   commitment of today?

2. One of the unique factors of Sarah's life is her isola-
   tion in the desert for many years. Read this description of the kind of land where she lived as a nomad,
   and draw conclusions about her development of
   faith.

   > At first sight the desert is a sad disappoint-
   > ment. . . . All looks like a gigantic vacant lot,
   > scrubby and dirty, lifeless and abandoned—miles
   > and miles of drab sameness. A few days later you
   > cannot imagine ever having this feeling. The des-
   > ert becomes a place of infinite change and subtlety,
   > alive and powerful. . . . Nowhere in the world
   > does the time of day make so great a difference to
   > the landscape. In early morning the sands are red
   > and vibrant . . . the air is cold, crisping the knife-
   > edge of the dune crests. . . . By ten o'clock it is hot
   > and the sun takes everything out of the desert.
   > There are no shapes, no shadows—only the shim-
   > mering streaks of the mirages. . . . Then it is dark,
   > suddenly and conclusively, and the desert ceases
   > to exist. There are only the stars—more vivid and
   > real than you have ever seen them. . . . The people
   > who live in this desert are as hard and spare as the

Redbook, February, 1975

land they inhabit, for to survive demands unrelenting attention and a rigid code of behavior. . . . Every attitude is geared to survival.**

**Howard Demton, *Saturday Evening Post*, Apr., 1974, p. 10.

3

Hannah: How To Have a Baby

Last year Harvard University's student spy report, "Configuide," ran an ad which began its pitch with these words: "When you want to know something, let's face it, you don't ask your mother. . . ."

As a mother reading those words (obviously not intended for my eyes) I asked myself, "Seriously now, why not?"

If you don't ask your mother, it's got to be for one of three reasons: (1) She doesn't know the answer; (2) She cannot be trusted to give you the right answer; (3) You have no communication with her.

Motherhood is God's invention. That a person should be the mechanical means of delivering another person to the human race is a profound and ingenious component of life. But in recent days the whole concept has been under attack. A high-toned, intellectual "roundtable" in Switzerland several years ago actually questioned whether mothers are necessary. Test tube babies, it felt, held the real promise for the future.

Some societies have felt that mothers should be screened. In our own western world there are those who feel a test should be devised so that only women with "inborn maternal instinct" should be allowed the privilege. Currently, the overpopulation problem has sparked the "two and no more" motto for parents.

Despite all the flak, motherhood is still getting some intelligent votes. Not smothering momism, nor the frigidity of the detached, career-lover who takes a quick maternity leave like an appendectomy absence but Motherhood with a capital M—the whole thing: body, soul, and spirit.

The most qualified voters are the children. They define motherhood as both a state of being and an action-packed vocation. Here's a colorful collage of young opinions:

> "A mother is the one who if she sings your favorite song it stops thundering."

> "Mothers always shout pick up your things and they mostly end up doing it themself."

> "If I forget to tell my mother I need my shepherd costume tomorrow morning, she finds one in the night. That is a mother!"

> "My mother, she's busy around Thanksgiving. By Christmas she's full of joy. By January she's even happier because school starts."

One anonymous sage wrote: "An ounce of mother is worth a pound of clergy." I always wondered if whoever said that had just read the book of 1 Samuel. It tells of a rather inelegant meeting of a would-be mother and a professional priest when the beginnings of a very notable life were decided. The woman's name was Hannah, and her desire for a son changed the course of the nation, Israel.

Application for Motherhood

Hannah and her husband, Elkanah, lived in the mildewed mixture of politics and religion which seesawed in the central highlands of Palestine at least a millenium before Christ. This husband was of priestly ancestry; he was a Levite, living in the territory of the tribe of Ephraim among the hills piled up between the Great Sea and the Jordan River. No land had been assigned to the tribe of Levi; God's plan was that they should live among the tribes in specified cities.

Hannah was caught in a domestic triangle, a three-sided marriage where she was loved by her husband but despised by the other wife.

Early Israel apparently practiced very little polygamy. Only Jacob and Gideon up to this point in the Bible are recorded as giving full wifehood status to more than one woman at a time.

Elkanah had two wives. Probably Hannah's infertility occasioned a second marriage to Peninnah who bore him children. Jewish survival demanded a high birth rate, a strong, growing nation.

American women tend to regard polygamy as simply a title in a sociology text, but for the wife who must live with other wives, days are cheerless and disillusioning. My memory stirs at this point to one of those rude shocks of reality which occurred when I visited Kenya in 1974.

I had addressed a short series of women's meetings at a church in the black section of Nairobi. Several days later a committee of leaders from this women's group called upon me to present a gift and to have tea. I am still moved as I reflect upon the generosity of those dear people, economically deprived, but full of a giving spirit. These women lived very spartan lives compared to mine. They were physically lean and muscular, weathered with hard work in and out of doors. But the glow of Christ's peace and love softened their weary faces.

We sat in a small circle and discussed our meetings through an interpreter. One of the leaders asked if she might present a prayer request. She came near to tears as she described a marital problem. Her husband had been a professing Christian, but now, unexpectedly, he had told her he was adding another wife to the family.

I am sure she saw the lack of comprehension in my eyes, although the other women registered immediate shock. I was too naive to understand, and so she attempted to explain through the language barrier that another wife would bring debasement in her home. She would be demoted, as it were. She, and especially her children, would suffer discrimination. She would get less to eat and more work to do, and life was already almost unbearable. How, she asked me, could Christ allow this to happen?

There have been many times in my life when I have had no answer—this was one of them. I simply bowed my head and said in my heart, "Oh God, there but for your grace, am I!" We prayed together and I felt like a kindergartner with graduate students in the college of experience. We laid it out before God and thanked Him that He "always leads us to triumph in Christ . . ." (2 Cor. 2:14).

Penninah taunted Hannah because of her barrenness. The writer of 1 Samuel says she "provoked her relentlessly." I once read a description of such a woman: "her faults were little faults and the scars accumulated like X-ray burns." It was not enough that Hannah suffered the unspoken humiliation of having no children; she also weathered a constant shower of petty criticism. There is no evidence that Hannah ever retorted. Undoubtedly she ached inside, but God often allows irritations to reveal His sufficiency. He is able to keep us going under the worst conditions.

A devout believer in Jehovah, Elkanah annually shepherded his family over the twelve-mile trip to worship at Shiloh, where they offered sacrifices according to the holy law. There the family worshiped Jehovah Sabaoth, the Lord of hosts. How pointless it must have seemed when their own nation was weak politically and the mighty Philistines periodically flexed their military muscles along the coastland. Canaanite idolatry was being accepted increasingly by the disunited Israelites and the priesthood was nearly powerless.

Hannah wanted a son. She had longed for this for years, but now her desire was uncontrollable and her sadness spilled over into weeping. Elkanah, like any loving, concerned husband, tried to comfort his meek, gentle-spirited wife. It was a problematic situation, but he was not driven to desperation. Hannah, on the other hand, was to the breaking point. She had a two-fold problem: personal and national—they both looked hopeless. The problem had piled up and overwhelmed her.

Elkanah applied typical masculine logic. He asked four questions: Why are you crying? Why are you not eating? Why is your heart grieved? Am I not better to you than ten sons?

Remember that this husband made no secret of the fact that he loved Hannah. With such emotional support, why would she cry? He had served to her, the record states, a worthy portion; that is, the choicest of food. With that in front of her, why couldn't she eat? Of course there was the matter of no children, but he had tried to make it up to her. Why couldn't she accept reality?

Hannah's desolation was peculiarly a woman's problem. How could a husband know the emptiness she felt in being denied the privilege of giving birth? How could he experience a loss of appetite over an empty nest? Did he share her fear for her people, God's chosen nation? Did he possess the sensitive insight to see the immoral eyes of the young priests as they went about their duties in the temple? Was he torn with terror over the obvious decay of their center of worship?

Prescription for Prayer

Hannah had a plan. To put it into action she left her plate apparently untouched and made her way to the post of the temple. This was not Solomon's temple of generations later, but it was the place of worship established by Joshua when the nation of Israel had taken possession of the land.

There Hannah prayed and wept. Many women do that, but she did one thing more. *She made a vow.* It could have been that up to this point her desire for a son was merely selfish and defensive, an effort to meet the competition under her own roof. Now her motive was altered. She exercised her will to ask for a son, not for herself but for the Lord God.

God's people have always struggled with this matter of talking to Him in prayer. Many feel there must be a key, certain words that unlock the Almighty's door. Why is it that some people seem to get so many answers and others seem to pray in vain?

There *is* a key to prayer. It shows up when we study the prayers of the Bible, especially in the Old Testament. They are based on pleas to God to keep His promises. He will always do that. This fact accounts for the many times the phrases "for Thy name's sake" and "according to Thy word" are used. In the New Testament, Peter says, "The Lord is not slow about His promises . . ." (2 Pet. 3:9). These prayers He delights to answer, but God does not indulge selfish whims.

I know this truth from personal experience. I once prayed for a house, but for the wrong reasons. I finally came to the point where I could say, "All right, Lord, if you want me to live here my whole life, I'm willing. I pray only for grace to do it." It was then that the Lord moved with amazing speed to change my situation. I knew unmistakably that my new home was His gift. It belonged to Him and was to be used for Him.

The decision to give her son back to God could not have been a spur-of-the-moment act of contrition. Otherwise she surely would have backed down when she found herself holding that long-awaited baby boy in her arms. Unquestionably, she had debated with herself and probed her own desires: why do you want this son?

Hannah's character is revealed to be totally honest. It is not difficult to see why Elkanah loved her. She was perceptive and courageous. Most importantly, she was full of faith, a reminder that "without faith it is impossible to please Him, for he who comes to God must believe that He is, and that He is a rewarder of those who seek Him" (Heb. 11:6). What a heritage to bequeath to her boy, a man whom God listed among the heroes of faith centuries later.

Hannah was hemmed in. We have all been there with her. Totally frustrated, unable to move. No exit. Dead ends. Let me give you an ultra-simple illustration.

Suppose I want to go somewhere. I need to go very

much, but I cannot get my car out of the garage. I have the car, the fuel, the license, and the know-how to drive, but remain boxed in. The door is shut. I can push and pull—even try to kick it open—but my little bit of strength and strategy with big doors is ridiculously mismatched. However, I have one bit of knowledge: this door which stands in the way between my imprisonment and my freedom is responsive to a higher source of power—electricity. Not just any application of electricity, but a formula, a wavelength worked out for my individual garage door. I press a button; the door opens . . . I am free.

So it is many times in life. I am hopelessly tied down with forces far beyond my moving. Yet deeply implanted in my heart is a release button. I have access to the power of all the universe. "Let us therefore draw near with confidence to the throne of grace, that we may receive mercy and may find grace to help in time of need" (Heb. 4:16).

Hannah prayed for a son with the holy intent of giving him as a living sacrifice to God. It is doubtful that she had any grandiose plan to save the nation. Like Mary breaking the alabaster box of ointment upon Christ, "she did what she could." God honored that step of faith.

In bitterness of soul, Hannah prayed. This same description was used of the woman of Shunem whose son died during the time of Elisha. She hit bottom—there was nothing left. Here is a familiar pattern: God allows His children to reach this nadir experience to demon strate His lifting power.

God's Nod of Approval

The decline of the clergy seems to jut out in the failure of the old priest Eli to recognize Hannah's true penitence. He mistook supplication for insobriety. It should be noted that prayer was usually offered audibly, but it was consonant with Hannah's nature not to verbalize this personal, intimate matter. Even as she held her tongue in anger and frustration with Peninnah, so she barely whispered her agony and hopes to Jehovah.

This praying woman had a concern that was national, but her immediate goal was personal. It involved God as the prime mover and herself as His tool. Her solution was invincible. Whatever the problem, the source of power must be adequate to solve it and the means of solving it must be available.

Eli the priest responded to this weeping, incoherent supplicant by granting a pious wish, not a deep prophetic request. The very fact that he suspected drunkenness reveals a low ebb of personal piety among the people. Nevertheless, God gave Hannah peace of heart. She left with her burden lifted. Her contract was with the Lord, not with the priest.

A Mother in Action

After the birth of Samuel, Hannah prayed a prayer of thanksgiving which helps us decipher her thinking. Her sonnet of praise moved in sharp contrast to her sadness before she turned her problem over to the Lord. Transfused with joy, she sketched a bold outline of God's holiness, His power, and His unchanging nature. Like a warrior charging into battle, she lashed at the proud, greedy, and wicked enemies of Israel who will be the objects of Jehovah's judgment. God sees everything, she announced, "For the Lord is a God of knowledge, and with Him actions are weighed." Her words are reminiscent of the writing on the wall at the feast of Belshazzer hundreds of years later: "You have

been weighed on the scales and found deficient" (Dan.
5:27).

The use of this imagery of the balance scale was
particularly pithy in ancient cultures. The Egyptian
Book of the Dead, for example, recorded that the heart
of a deceased person is weighed on the scale against the
symbol of Truth and Right before he is admitted to the
Realm of Isiris.

The place of the Hebrew woman in these early days is
also noteworthy. This biblical narrative shows Hannah
to be her own woman. In conversations with her husband and with the priest, she was treated as an equal.
Later, when the child was born, the decision of when to
go to Shiloh was entirely Hannah's. Even the naming of
the baby seems to have been influenced by his mother.

Whenever God deals with women, He acts in tender
respect and loving protection. As a wife, Hannah most
certainly bowed to her husband's wishes, but there
was obviously a mutual esteem. "Do what seems best
to you. Remain until you have weaned him . . ."
(1 Sam. 1:23). Elkanah's response to his wife shows
high regard for her, for his son, and for his own confidence in God's future guidance.

Keeping the baby Samuel at home until he was
weaned would traditionally mean several years, possibly as many as four or five. Elkanah readily agreed with
the decision to allow Samuel to remain at home with
his mother until that time. Then, in fidelity to their
word, the parents appeared together before Eli, bringing the slain animal along when the child was presented. "So I have also dedicated him to the Lord; as
long as he lives he is dedicated to the Lord" (1 Sam.
1:28). These are the words of Hannah, fully legal and
acceptable in this patriarchal society.

This was the moment of truth for Hannah. The intensity of her faith glows from the page as one reads of her

placing this young, impressionable boy in the hands of Eli, a man she most certainly knew to be an unworthy and incapable father. There was no hesitation; she and God understood each other.

Henry Ward Beecher once said that a mother's heart is the child's schoolroom. At least during those first formative years, Samuel undoubtedly learned his spiritual ABCs from the godly Hannah. Modern researchers tell us a child's emotional framework is formed by the time he is three years old. The divine launching pad was well chosen in the design for Israel's future leader.

When Hannah had left young Samuel in the temple, she sang aloud an outburst of praise, the overflow of a liberated heart. As surely as the dawn follows the darkness, God gives joy and freedom to those who give their best to Him.

Returning home with her husband, Mother Hannah now began the routine of loving her little son at a distance. Any mother can attest to the strain, the questions: Does he miss me? Will he manage all right by himself? Will he get homesick? Will he eat as he should? Will he stay covered when he is asleep? One can only guess the number of times she talked to God about her boy.

Every year there was mounting eagerness as the time came to visit Shiloh. Anticipation? Yes, but perhaps also a trace of anxiety. Surely Hannah knew, as all who worshiped at the temple must have known, that Eli's sons were wicked men. They seduced the women worshipers and feasted on the food given for sacrifice. What sort of influence would they have on the innocent Samuel?

Such matters would be resolved by God. Hannah had her agreement settled with God. She was now bearing other children and preparing each year for the return visit to the temple. Her maternal love was poignantly recorded in the words, "his mother would make him a little robe, and bring it to him from year to year. . . ." (1 Sam. 2:19). This robe was one of distinction, commonly worn by kings, prophets, and other people of position and rank. With a handmade emblem of her faith, it was evident that she saw her son as an honored servant of Jehovah.

Whenever a child of God stretches himself out in total belief, he is rewarded many times over. Having given Samuel entirely and irrevocably to the Lord, Hannah was given five additional children. "He is a rewarder of those who seek Him" (Heb. 11:6).

Motherhood—Is It Worth It?

In the hot and cold of Hannah's life, God spaded, seeded, and germinated His provision for His people. Children are a reward, says the psalmist; they are arrows in the hands of parents to be launched toward a worthy target (Psalm 127).

Many young women of this decade have asked me, "Why have kids? I mean, it's like there is no tomorrow. This is a crummy world. I don't think it's worth it. When I think of what my parents went through . . . and it's getting worse!"

Have we reached the point where we can say, "Let's call it quits"? No. Pharaoh was throwing Hebrew babies into the Nile River when Moses was born. Herod was murdering every male child of two years and under after God's own Son was born. History in the past has been painted in much darker hues than we see today. God is perfectly capable of growing young lives to worthwhile adults. But the lessons of the past teach us that parents must be serious about the task.

At a June, 1976, commencement ceremony, a

graduating law student addressed her audience of career-minded men and women:

> I . . . will address myself to the changes that have come over me and my friends . . . in the real world. Last year on my fifth reunion (of undergraduate college) the problem on everyone's mind was that of career versus family. Could one have a loving husband, children, and *two* successful and fulfilling careers? . . . . I stand before you today, law degree practically in hand, mother of two glorious children, and I bring you bad news: it will be a long time before the needs of family and career will be comfortably wed. . . . Child raising is important work. It has its moment of unequalled joy. It is also difficult and time-consuming. Yet child raising is not a respected profession . . . if my own experience means anything I cannot overstate how difficult it is to do justice to both children and a career. It is a constant battle.[1]

Any mother who has tried to work outside the home while rearing a family will honestly admit that most often it is the children who are shortchanged in favor of the job. Must we always vote in favor of the moment, when values of life and eternity are at stake?

My mind reaches back to a popular thesis offered by B. F. Skinner famed for his book *Beyond Freedom and Dignity*. "We can explain human behavior in terms of human responses; that is, reward or pain," he said in a television interview. When asked if moral attitudes in society are entirely shaped by external factors, Dr. Skinner replied, "Yes, the statement is essentially correct."

"How, then, do you account for the phenomenon of the family?" the commentator asked.

Skinner's answers included genetic environment, evolution of maternal behavior, and the inbuilt tendency to operate for the good of others as well as ourselves.[2]

Such lofty words do not even resemble what I am seeing. Alcoholic, drug-addicted, divorced mothers. Runaways. Abortions. Suicides.

Motherhood is suffering from a bad press. We have earned it. *Good Housekeeping* recently carried an article occasioned by response to a previously published letter about a young couple getting themselves "childproofed." The letter brought more than 10,000 responses, of which 70 percent said they would *not* have any children if they had it to do over again.

Clearly, we have made a mess of parenthooood. With more books, articles, courses, and experts on family life infiltrating American life than ever before, we continue to flounder. Perhaps we are giving the wrong advice. Consider this:

> A person doesn't have to make a full-time career of being a parent in order to help shape a child's character, even in the first two or three years. . . . the person substituting for the parents may frequently speak to the child of the importance of measuring up to the parents' expectations. . . . The care of children isn't just creative; it's delightful if you've developed the taste for it. (Tastes are acquired, whether for olives or gold or pantsuits.)[3]

Children are not things to be acquired and used or set aside for personal satisfaction. We have shamelessly devalued our children. We herd them into child-care centers like cars in a parking lot. We have devised all sorts of disguises so we can hide from them when they have problems. As we grow older, we see them as rivals and we teach them by example how to withdraw by getting instead of giving, and then to wither and to die in loneliness.

Hannah was a woman of vision. God fulfilled His

purpose through her seeing eyes. She lived in a day of darkness—personally, politically, and spiritually. She had no means to solve her problems by herself. She was not beautiful, nor rich, nor influential. She had only one thing—a belief in a God who cared. ''The Lord is near to the brokenhearted, and saves those who are crushed in spirit''(Ps. 34:18).

But her belief went beyond mere theory. She acted upon it. ''The Lord is near to all who call upon Him, to all who call upon Him in truth'' (Ps. 145:18).

God's etching of the model mother looks remarkably like Hannah. She knows the answers in life because she knows the Giver of life. She can be trusted to give the right answer because her relationship is one of love, of intelligent caring.

Every day the newspaper carries obituaries, reminders that life has ended for more people. Read them and remember that the only living thing they can leave is the children who live on after them.

Study Questions: Chapter 3

1. Read 2 Kings 4:8–37. Compare the woman of Shunem with Hannah. What principles may we draw about God's dealing with motherhood?

2. According to 1 Sam. 8:1–5, Samuel's sons were inadequate spiritual leaders. What principles of leadership were ignored and/or pursued by Samuel and his national leaders? Is Hannah in any way responsible for the defection of her grandsons?

4

Naomi: Major League Mother-in-law

Nellie wandered through childhood like a piece of human flotsam. Her mother had been a barmaid, rearing her little girl from town to town, wherever she could get hired to pour and mix drinks. As a teen-ager, Nellie was propelled into the stream of rootless, immoral living in a struggle to survive. She washed up on the shores of a barstool in Florida.

The bleary-eyed man beside her muttered, "Ah-m lookin' fer the mos' rotten, low-down, wicked woman ah c'n fine—d'yew knew where I c'n find one?"

Shifting from her own shell of misery, Nellie replied, "You're a-lookin' right at 'er! You won't find nobody worse'n me!"

It was a year later when Nellie told me this story. She and her drinking buddy, who is now her husband, had both reached the bottom. Neither of them had any money, family, or resources of any kind, and they ended up standing on a strange doorstep begging something to eat. The only thing they had in common was heartache. He was a race-car driver. His up-and-down marriage had crashed. The last spark of self-respect had flickered when his wife ran off with another driver—a man of criminal record and evil reputation. In his anger and humiliation, he determined to drown himself in degradation.

When Nellie and her companion knocked on that strange door, little did they know that a hand would reach out, not only to their bodies, but to their souls as well. A loving couple took them in, sheltered them, nurtured them, and introduced them to the Bread of Life.

The worst that this world can offer is no match for God's ability to restore and mend a broken life. Naomi, the Old Testament woman of what our world would call "rotten luck," found God merciful, just as Nellie did. But, unlike Nellie, Naomi started out with promise.

The Grass Is Always Greener. . .

Naomi and Elimelech were moving, leaving Bethlehem-Judah, the thriving agricultural center which later earned fame as the birthplace of Jesus Christ. Could this possibly be the Promised Land? Had not Jehovah promised to bring His people into a land of wheat and barley, of olive oil and honey? Had not Moses himself said it would be ". . . a land where you shall eat food without scarcity . . ." (Deut. 8:9)?

Elimelech ("God is king") must have harbored strong doubts about his heritage. Parched barley fields surrounded him; dry creekbeds stood in quiet dejection. The Promised Land, scene of highest hopes and heady victories for Joshua, the great general, was now a near-wasteland. Bethlehem, the granary of the nation, was now a weary outpost of survival. In a state of decay, the shriveled heirs of God's promises were scattered and discouraged; "every man did what was right in his own eyes."

What must have been Naomi's hopes and fears as she packed for her husband and their two young sons, closed up the house, and set out? Like many others before them and since, they wanted to make a new start. Naomi and Elimelech joined a trickle of refugees moving down into the Moabite hills where plentiful rains fed the Arnon River and the people prospered. Alien territory loomed ahead. Here Eglon, Moab's ruler, had in former years allied himself with local Bedoins and marched boldly into Benjamite territory, only to lose his life with ten thousand of his men in the attempt. It was in this region where the Israelite judge, Jephthah, had haggled with the Ammonites on the north bank of the bordering Arnon River.

Would the people be friendly to a family from Judah? I suspect that personal survival—perhaps even stubborn resentment—shadow?d Elimelech's fears, and even his religious convictions. He had had it with Judah and was willing to make concessions in order to find a productive farm.

"It's just temporary," they must have said to each other. Israelites would rarely forsake their land. Certainly they intended to return after the famine passed and the boys—Mahlon ("weak") and Chilion ("wasting")—had regained their strength. But here the high green meadows and the arable fields spawned prospect for a new start in life.

Interlude of Disillusionment

To Naomi it must have seemed a fresh release as they eluded the choking dust of Canaan. Even the sweaty, toilsome work of cultivating fields held the promise of harvest. Surely here the children would grow stronger.

Although the famine was behind them, Naomi and Elimelech faced a new shortage—a spiritual drought:

Their Moabite neighbors worshiped the heathen god Chemosh. Child sacrifice was the hallmark. To the Israelite mind human life was precious, and they must have shuddered to witness the pagan rites. You can almost see the four of them offering their animals on the simple altar as Moses had commanded. For this family there could be no idolatry. Their neighbors, undoubtedly, looked on with interest at these strange newcomers.

Light shines brightest in the darkness. Most probably this Israelite home was a focal point of interest in the community. But the family had not been settled long before death snatched away Elimelech. With sad and heavy hearts the young men and their mother buried him in the strange land. To be away—far away—from the family and the priest at this crucial time added to the sorrow. But Naomi picked up the broken strands of her life and continued to lead her home in the faithful worship of Jehovah.

As Mahlon and Chilion grew into manhood, they took wives. Orpah and Ruth, two young women born outside the circle of God's promises, were now drawn into the warmth of a home where Jehovah—that great and terrible God whom all the world knew had delivered the Israelite nation out of Egypt—was believed and obeyed. Levitical law did not prohibit such marriages. Orthodox relatives and friends at home would have frowned, but legally only heathen males were barred from the congregation.

For Orpah and Ruth this home stood apart from other Moabite dwellings. Honesty, purity, and mutual respect of parents and children—these hallmarks of the Hebrew home must have beckoned to these two young women and generated a belief in Jehovah when they were invited to become a legal part of Elimelech's family.

Nothing speaks more eloquently to a stranger than warm, loving acceptance. I vividly recall moving to Fort Worth, Texas, as a new pastor's wife. My eastern city roots were still showing in speech, attitudes, and a secret disdain for this slow, homespun mentality.

I soon learned, however, that I was the unsophisticate. My frantic and often superficial pace of living was like spinning wheels. My snap judgments were no match for the sane, prudent decisions which brought these people not only more prosperity than I had ever seen, but a certain *joie de vivre* that was delightfully contagious. These marvelously magnetic "strangers" knew how to live. Moreover, they accepted me, loved me, and converted me into a contented Texan!

Ruth and Orpah must have had the same experience. They were loved by Naomi and her sons. What a crushing blow it was when their means of livelihood faded! Like an uninvited intruder, death brooded over the home. Elimelech, the head, the breadwinner, was gone. Numbing reality surely gripped Naomi as she nurtured and clung to her two sons, who were both apparently in poor health. But all her nursing knowledge, the wholesome food, the fresh air, and the motherly devotion were futile in the brutal battle with disease. Ten years after leaving Bethlehem-Judah, Naomi was not only a grieving widow, but a mother without sons.

The triple deaths in the family, so full of struggling hope for the future, had reduced Naomi to a posture of poverty and destitution. For the second time in her life all means of support seemed to be gone. Before, there had been the love and warmth of the family. Now she was alone. Ruth and Orpah were fine young women, but what could they do . . . really?

Some people seem to hang on in the centrifuge of a collapsed life. Others are flung, fragmented, into destruction. Television in recent years has brought a stark contrast between the ways two American families handle problems. We have all loved the story of the Waltons; real people—pious, hardworking, and unpretentious. Breathing economically thin air, they navigated with skill and satisfaction the depression years. They had no shiny appliances, fancy cars, stereos or swimming pools, but the three-generation family poured out their lives for each other and for those in their community. The rewards were rich—and it was fiction.

In contrast, "An American Family" was reality. The Loud family dared to permit the eye of the camera into their home. We all viewed ourselves through them—our compulsion to entertain each other, our occupation with trivia. Near the end of the series a divorce was imminent; the family was fractured.

"That's too bad," we all said. A moment of regret was the most we could give. We wanted to forgive and forget. How often we want to dismiss other people's sorrow with a flick of sympathy and go on. No time, really, to get involved.

I think Naomi sensed this normal tendency to dissociate from the unfortunate person. "I don't want your bad luck to rub off on me," some would think. Naomi understood that Ruth and Orpah would naturally want to go back to their familiar surroundings. What reason did they have to stay when their husbands were gone?

The tragedy forced difficult decisions. Ruth and Orpah had probably severed relations with their own heathen families, having stepped into the light of belief in Jehovah and the respect accorded to Jewish women. To return to their Moabite families would mean not only criticism and a return to lower status, but also probably another marriage.

Naomi herself had nothing to offer them, she reasoned. The loss of any one of her men would have been a disaster, but the stripping away of all three left her with an anguish and grief indescribable. Certainly there was no visible income.

Have you ever talked with someone who is alone and hurting badly? What happens in the office when the salesman who was always such a fun person stops at your desk with a dejected look?

"What's the matter," you ask.

"Listen, I've got to tell somebody—I'm in trouble—my marriage is coming unglued—I . . . I really don't know what to do—I've always thought of you as a friend . . ."

"Oh, gee, I'm sorry," you reply. "I really am. Maybe you ought to go see a counselor—you know, somebody who knows about those things. . . ." in other words, don't stop here; I don't have any answers. And then you chuckle and try to send him on with a smile.

"Well, don't let it get you down! At least you have lots of company these days!"

"Yeah, well . . . ah . . . thanks. I really didn't mean to bother you." He flicks his cigarette ashes and moves away. He's reading your mind—you've tossed him in with all the other losers. He walks away, wishing his nightmare would be over. But it isn't.

Like wreckage floating from a devastating storm, the widows apparently buried their dead, closed their home, and approached the dreaded moment of separation. Naomi insisted the young women return to their mothers' homes. Was it out of love or desperation? As Naomi experienced a sense of weak helplessness, she expected each of the girls to feel the same. Where else to go but back home?

The suggestion had merit, for the heathen oriental cultures, although they held no status for women, did provide women's quarters. The quarters were presided over by the mother and they afforded protection as well as opportunity for marriage.

With rational planning and confidence in God, Naomi surveyed the scene wisely and realistically. She was sorrowful, but she summoned reserves of strength and stamina.

I have come to believe that part of the answer to why God brings tragedy and overwhelming problems into our lives is to force us to exercise abilities we never use. My mother, for example, became a different woman after Dad died. It was excruciating for all of us, but especially for her, to drag through ten months of watching Dad waste away from a virile, active, working man to an atrophied, pain-racked victim of cancer.

Having spent every available dollar in a vain attempt to save his life, she was forced to say good-bye, and she buried him. Exhausted and in need of surgery herself, she lay in a hospital bed and asked the Lord to take her also. The future was bleak and visible resources were non-existent.

Instead, God pointed her to Himself. He restored her health and gave her training and a job which she had never dreamed possible. He can and does make the lame to walk again. "Those who wait for the Lord will gain new strength; they will mount up with wings like eagles, they will run and not get tired, they will walk and not become weary" (Isa. 40:31).

Naomi is living proof that God never forsakes those who trust Him. His wisdom is their portion, the wisdom that is "from above." James says (3:17) that it is first pure, then peaceable, gentle, reasonable. . . . Her motives were just and her method was to do what was right for each of her daughters. For herself, she had to return to Judah. She was finding her way, as do wounded things in the woods, to the place where she was born.

Orpah's decision to return to her mother's home was sound. She would lose honor and position as a Jewish wife, but bereavement had come at an early age. Respecting Naomi's judgment, she returned to become eligible again for marriage and motherhood.

Ruth, whose name means "a friend," could not be dissuaded. Refusing to bow to the ravages of circumstance, she responded instead to Naomi's strength. Her reply to Naomi's plea to return is poignant poetry.

While her filial love must have warmed Naomi's heart, it also bred uncertainty. Did Naomi really want responsibility for this young life? Certainly she welcomed the companionship, but bringing an immigrant home was risky.

Ruth's avowal of faith in Jehovah sealed the agreement. The touching quality of Ruth's decision lies in her settled heart. She did not ask or plead for understanding. She simply stated her intentions: "Do not urge me to leave you or turn back from following you; for where you go, I will go, and where you lodge, I will lodge. Your people shall be my people, and your God, my God. Where you die, I will die, and there I will be buried" (Ruth 1:16,17).

Ruth's words indicate that she had thought through the implications for leaving her homeland. She had cast her vote not so much with this individual whom she had come to love and respect, but with Naomi's God, her people, and their land. She sensed an eternal dimension to Naomi's faith that transcended even her deepest heartaches. The life of her mother-in-law reflected a personal tie with the supernatural. Clearly God Himself had changed Ruth's heart; she was a true believer.

Although she had never seen it, the strange land of Canaan drew Ruth like a magnet. It was not only the home of those whom she had come to love, but it was the vortex of this life-changing faith that stood in stark contrast to all her heathen background. She was willing to give up her name, her citizenship, her very identity to be numbered as a proselyte Jewess. Her conversion was complete and genuine because Naomi had lived a miracle.

Some months ago the syndicated columnist Carl Rowan wrote a tribute to his mother-in-law, who had died at age ninety. Having been reared in slave country, she married a humble man but retained lifelong pride and self-esteem. "I would give a week of my salary every month to anyone," said Mr. Rowan, "with a successful formula for creating throughout black America the sense of family, the quest for achievement, the respect for learning, the motivation of children. . . ."[1] that his parents-in-law produced. It was something of this uncommon motivation which Naomi exuded, I believe, that ignited Ruth.

Promised Land Revisited

Have you ever wondered what Ruth and Naomi discussed on their journey to Bethlehem? It was a long way to walk, or even to ride by donkey—possibly as much as a hundred miles. They could not know they were following the escape route from personal disaster. No light shone at the end of the tunnel.

> Luck did not change the plight of thousands of innocent victims of Nazi oppression. They went to their death— there was no answer for them in the back of the book. Destiny cannot be left to find its own mooring; it must be hitched to an all-wise Person.[2]

These words, written about World War II, could be the epitaph of many in history. Life or death, as the case may be, must be decided by God. Naomi and Ruth had little to go on—only a brief news report that the famine was past, that there was bread in the "House of Bread."

A decade earlier the road out of Bethlehem had been for Naomi a yellow brick road leading to adventure and escape from hardship. Now, as Naomi and Ruth turned their faces again toward the town that Naomi had tried to bury in her past, the sights along the way must have marched in her memory like an old faded movie reel playing backwards.

Naomi reached Bethlehem, bringing Ruth with her. To her hometown relatives and friends she spoke not merely of Jehovah, but she credited the choreographer of her life, *El Shaddai*, the Almighty. She was saying that God was the strengthener and satisfier of His people; literally, the strong-breasted One, the all-sufficient One, who not only enriches, but makes fruitful. This was the same name God had revealed to Abraham when he was ninety years old and His covenant was re-confirmed. Naomi's body was aged, but her spirit was renewed. She could not have talked to El Shaddai without a hint of hope for the future.

"Call me Mara," she said, which means "bitter." On the calendar of her culture, Naomi was an old woman. She may have been only in her forties, but heartache and disappointment had grayed her hair and wrinkled her skin. Care and poverty had stooped her shoulders and dimmed the light in her eyes as she lived through the wanderings in her own personal wilderness.

Naomi, in referring to "Mara," recalled the disillusionment of her people years before. When the Israelites had escaped the horses and chariots of the Egyptian army, Moses' sister Miriam had taken timbrel in hand and led the women in singing and dancing over the Lord's deliverance. But as the company grew tired and thirsty, the melodrama of the Red-Sea escape had sifted into the sand. A welcome oasis had appeared on the horizon and the travelers had hurried to reach the water and quench their thirst. But it was bitter. They could not drink it and they named it Marah.

Reflecting on Naomi's life, it is important to note that God's dealing with her was not necessarily a consequence of sin or disobedience. In the wilderness, God was not punishing his newly liberated people. He was simply teaching them their true source of supply: "My help comes from the Lord, who made heaven and earth" (Ps. 121:1).

"Mara." Bitter. Naomi's word described to her people a whole story, a decade of trial. She had returned thirsty—personally and spiritually. She had traveled to Moab with high hopes, but found it bitter. Her spirit was crushed.

In the wilderness the people had "grumbled at Moses, saying, "What shall we drink?" Then he cried out to the Lord, and the Lord showed him a tree; and he threw it into the waters, and the waters became sweet . . ." (Ex. 15:24-25). As it had been with the nation, now it happened with Naomi. Her sense of vertical direction was still intact, and *El Shaddai*, the covenant-keeping God, once again proved Himself adequate and faithful.

One of the most common problems of ageing is hopelessness. I wonder how often the question has been asked, "Why did God let this happen to me?" Ill health, financial ruin, loss of a partner—some irretrievable resource gone. We instinctively feel that as long as we have our youth, we can possibly make it, but when we are deprived of physical capability, we tend to give up. We fail to see that when the flesh is helpless the spirit can be strong if it relies upon God's Spirit. We are most susceptible to God's working when we have given up and He can show us His power.

At the old Mission House in Honolulu I descended a flight of stairs into a darkened cellar. There the early missionaries had built their kitchen to escape the heat of the tropics. At the bottom of the stairs was a large stone, a piece of lava rock hollowed out where water was filtered in the early days.

When the missionaries arrived, so full of concern for the spiritual welfare of the Hawaiians, they were received coolly; they were allowed to stay, but consigned to the swamplands in the area which is now Honolulu. The only water available was brackish, unfit to drink. Ingeniously they devised this purification of their drinking water, although it was agonizingly slow; something like one-half cup per hour dripped through the rock. A canal was built to drain the land and purify the springs. What had looked like an unlivable situation began to take the shape of desirable property. God made a way where there appeared to be no way for His servants.

Ruth, the brave and noble daughter-in-law, stands in history as living proof of God's provision for Naomi. She rises from the pages of Scripture to become the heroine to all who read this intriguing tale. But Naomi was the seed—spiritually speaking—from which Ruth sprang.

In many ways the mother-daughter linkup is a strange connection. We all need and want to be mothered—to have an older, wiser, soft touch to soothe and sustain our spirits. But rare is the woman who can reach out, without holding on, to a grown daughter (or daughter-in-law). To tell a younger woman what to do, when, in effect, that younger woman is competing for your place is next to impossible.

A friend once told me: "My daughters personify all that I used to be. Sometimes I'm ashamed to say, I almost hate them. They have the beautiful skin, the firm, well-shaped bodies, the flush of youthful beauty. They are "with it" in terms of our society—aware, alert, attractive to the male members of the family. I find myself standing on the second row in the family pictures, sitting in the back seat of the car, increasingly voting with the minority opinion in family matters."

Blending into the background in deference to a new "front and center" is not easy. Let us not think Naomi and Ruth did not have to deal with some of these sticky matters.

Our society has brainwashed us with the falsehood that old women are useless. So often, when they can no longer work the eight-to-five shift, or at least run the vacuum cleaner, we set them in a rocking chair in front of the television set. There their minds become removed from reality, duped, and deteriorated. We feed them tranquilizers, waiting for some vital organ to lapse, hoping they will slip away "without suffering." What a waste of wisdom and vitality!

Money Matters

And just as Naomi experienced the extremes of economic pressures, so have many of us. We have known what it is to be short on funds, perhaps down to our last cent. And at some time we have read the words of Paul, "I know how to get along with humble means, and I also know how to live in prosperity . . ." (Phil. 4:12). And we say—Yes, Paul, I know what you mean. I've been there, too.

But have we *really*? Paul did not say "I have *experienced* poverty or plenty . . ." He said "I know *how* . . ."

There's a difference. I believe Naomi caught that difference. You see, the question is not how much money we have—actually, that's God's business. He gives. He takes away. He supplies all our needs. He's pledged Himself to do that. Christ said the lilies of the field and the sparrows of the air—lesser creations than man—are well taken care of, and we will be, too. The question is not *how much*, but *how*!

How do we handle lack of money? Or enough of money? Or too much of money? It's our *attitude* that God records. Lack of worry, absence of fretting, a spirit of thankfulness, whatever the supply; this is pleasing to Him.

Naomi was caught in the vice of grinding poverty—and it is a vice. It seemed that all her resources had evaporated. She probably had just enough money to get back to Bethlehem. And possibly, Ruth's insistence in accompanying her posed an embarrassment. Maybe Ruth was penniless too and Naomi would have to share her meager rations—hardly enough for one, let alone two.

Then there was that sticky matter of bringing an alien Moabite into a town where there might be racial prejudice. Ruth was the living, breathing evidence that Elimilech's boys had married outside the faith. Everybody in town would see Naomi's worn clothes and haggard body. It was humiliating.

Let's admit honestly that when Naomi and Ruth got back to Bethlehem, Naomi did not have the "Pauline perspective"! She could not see, as he did, "For momentary, light affliction is producing for us an eternal weight of glory far beyond all comparison" (2 Cor. 4:17). It is not recorded that she told Ruth or anybody else "Rejoice in the Lord always; again I will say, rejoice!" as Paul did from behind prison bars (Phil. 4:4).

No, instead she asked that her very name be changed from Naomi, meaning *pleasant,* to Mara, which means "bitter."

But Naomi was honest. The bitterness of her experience never embittered her spirit against God. She bowed to His control of her life. She "took it" with a submissive spirit.

Naomi's Lantern Relit

Naomi had a whole new life ahead in Bethlehem. With spiritual perception, she saw the means for new, green growth through the grafting of Ruth into her family tree. The women who had formed the wide-eyed welcoming committee upon Naomi's return from Moab now witnessed God at work in the soil of re-cultivated life. God gave Naomi a new family. "Blessed is the Lord who has not left you without a redeemer today. . . . may he also be to you a restorer of life and a sustainer of your old age; for your daughter-in-law, who loves you and is better to you than seven sons, has given birth to him" (Ruth 4:14–15).

"A son has been born to Naomi. . . ." Her identity was restored; her heart and home were healed. Did she, possibly, look into the face of her beautiful grandson and think of how close she had come to ditching the whole thing? Back there in Moab when all had seemed irrevocably lost, she had clung desperately to the only thing she had left—a belief in an eternal God. When all else was gone, it was the only shred of essence that mattered. I am sure she sang the words of Moses:

Who is like Thee among the gods,
  O Lord?
Who is like Thee, majestic in holiness,
Awesome in praises, working wonders? . . .

In Thy lovingkindness Thou hast led the people whom
Thou hast redeemed;
In Thy strength Thou hast guided them to Thy holy
habitation. . . .
Thou wilt bring them and plant them in the mountains of
Thine inheritance. . . .
The Lord shall reign forever and ever.

(Exodus 15)

Study Questions: Chapter 4

1. Possibly more than any other woman in the Bible, Naomi forces us to consider the subject of death and loss. Dr. Elizabeth Kubler-Ross, contemporary researcher on this subject, has described five stages of dying patients: denial (it can't be true), anger (why me?), bartering (just a little more time), depression, and resignation.

   Compare Paul's commentary on death (1 Cor. 15:13–22; 53–58; 1 Thess. 4:13,14) with this analysis and with Naomi's experiences. What attitudes should we ourselves cultivate?

2. The original recipients of the letter to the Hebrews in the New Testament were partners in poverty with Elimelech's family in Ruth. To them these words were written (10:35,36):

   Therefore, do not throw away your confidence, which has a great reward. For you have need of endurance, so that when you have done the will of God, you may receive what was promised.

   What does this teach us about poverty, ill health, and loss?

5
Love Fit For a King

Last night was our twelfth wedding anniversary. I thought I would surprise my husband, so I sent the children to their grandmother's, worked like a demon cleaning the house, and prepared a gourmet meal. When my husband got home, I greeted him with a cocktail and wished him happy anniversary. He was upset that he had forgotten but instead of being pleased with everything I had done, he was sulky and irritable. After dinner he just sat and watched television and I went to bed, crying myself to sleep.[1]

This plaintive peek into a wife's personal life depicts a plight not uncommon in our world—rejected love. Counselors today are deluged with laments of marriage partners who are distressed because their love has been trampled. Whatever the crosswinds in this particular example—selfish manipulation, insensitivity to outside tensions—obviously the whole story is not told—an eager spirit is reaching out to another, and has been bruised.

The inner self (where we all live) is in reality fragile and easily damaged. Its texture is so minutely complex that to explain it in words is nearly impossible. Who can adequately describe the gossamer wisp of feelings which are damaged by a look, a word, or a movement, yet which are powerful enough to steer a life, a family, or a nation? The Bible, in the refined rendition of King Solomon's love story, wraps it in a sheer film of poetry.

If a hard-nosed producer of American television were to look at the Song of Solomon as potential "property," I suspect he would discard it after a casual reading. Perhaps he would scrawl across its face "not enough suspense," "no grit," or "where's the crunch?"

An addition of "realism" would, no doubt, be suggested, for we moderns have come not only to wink at wickedness in our so-called "love" relationships, but to welcome an injection of evil and infidelity. I recall a ditty from some distant source:

> Everywhere I look I see—
> Fact or fiction, life or play—
> Still the little game of Three
> B and C in love with A.

We relish the triangular drama; we revel in lust; we crow over having outgrown the happily-ever-after endings.

In our own personal lives, however, we long for a steady stream of support and accommodation from those nearest us. " 'Til death do us part" is still the ideal for which we yearn. We want to be loved—with no competition, no interruption, and no rejection. Such love the Song describes.

Taking the Shulamite's Pulse

The poetry of the Song is complex, reflecting ancient Eastern culture. A study of its structure and meaning is best left to those scholars with Hebraic and historical expertise. But as a contemporary western-world woman, I want to look at this Shulamite woman. If she was not only worthy of the attention of Solomon, the wisest man who ever lived, but also deserving of a niche in the writings of the Old Testament, then I want to take her pulse. Surely she has much to teach me about giving and receiving love. In my crass, mechanistic world, I need all the help I can get.

As if unpacking a dusty old chest in the attic, I feel the need to see Solomon's Song in the daylight of modern phraseology, in order to import to me over this wide linguistic gulf the onrush of feeling and the depth of passion I find packed away.

This woman's actual identity, according to some scholars, could have been Absihag of Shunem. If so, then she was the beautiful young virgin who was brought into the chambers of the aged King David, as recorded in the opening verses of 1 Kings, and who moved on after David's death to become Solomon's wife.

It is enough to know that she actually did exist and that the Holy Spirit elevates her physical beauty to the importance of recording its effect on King Solomon. Such divine attention to good looks encourages me. It tells me He has given me whatever glamour, sex appeal, or comeliness that I may have as a resource, an asset to be used. The question is *how*?

I once talked with a friend who had been voted a campus beauty at her college alma mater. Enlarged photos of her were displayed in the campus paper, the student union bulletin boards, the local photographer's window, and numerous other locations. Naturally, she was very popular with the young men; they almost stood in line just to be her escort for a single event.

"What is it like to be indescribably beautiful?" I had always wanted to ask that question.   ,

"Well, I'd be lying if I didn't say it was kind of exciting at first. Of course, my parents helped me to take it in stride." (As a mother, I could relate to the importance of her parents.)

"But then it got so I almost wished I were ugly. Men can be so cheap. I was really glad when I got married." Today she is loved and adored by a husband and three wonderful children. Her secret is that she does not think of herself as a great beauty, but rather as an asset to the lifetime lover and companion God has given her.

My own husband and I have made a kind of private survey of the many women we have met over the years and we agree that by far the most beautiful women we know are the well-loved wives—in all age brackets. Charm and beauty are temporary, we are told in Proverbs 31:30. They cannot last on their own, but when they are invested in the life of another, they are solidified in a very real sense. The protection and care of a loving husband is probably the very best preservative.

What can I learn from Solomon's portrait of his beloved? This inspired lyric crystallizes at least six approaches to love which are expressed in the quotations of the lovers.

SENSITIVITY: Like my African violets which keep turning and reaching for the sunlight, this young fiancée stretches every fibre of her being in the direction of her lover. She tunes out nearly everybody else—certainly any other suitor—to focus on him. In the description, every one of their five senses is employed.

Hearing: She hears his voice, catching every nuance, studying every word, every pause, replaying it in her mind when he is away. The lover who listens is the lover who reads accurately her personal incoming lovegrams.

Seeing: She sees him, his whole splendid physical body, and loves everything she sees. It fits perfectly into the entire scheme of God's masterful creation. There are more than twenty references in the Song to plants and animals of nature, but the human body excels them all. The sight of him excites her desire to fondle him.

Touching: With infinite variety the sensation of touch surfaces in the music of these lines, provoking questions about wifely behavior. How tightly does she hold him? How long? How frequently? With what part of her anatomy? Hair? Smooth palm? Bony elbow? What about warmth? Moisture? The soft brush of an eyelash? The feel of a cold nose? Hot breath? A fingernail lightly on the skin? His foot playfully tripping her into his arms? The press of his kiss on her lips? It is found from the beginning of the first chapter through the last. There is no end to the tenderness of touch. Its message transcends words.

Taste: She eats and drinks with him, sharing the delicate flavors and pungent seasonings of their common food. And in those deepest, most intimate moments together, she touches his body with her tongue and finds him sweet.

Smell: Her body is clean, constantly annointed with sweet-smelling spices and perfumes, always appealing, always wafting a message for him: come. The intricate network bonding the two lovers forms a strong mutual admiration and simple delight in each other's presence. Through innumerable nuances of feeling they move toward each other: "I am my beloved's, and his desire is for me" (Song 7:10).

EAGERNESS: This sparkling young woman projects a verve that stimulates her lover. The opening verses show this: "Draw me after and let us run together" (Song 1:4). She is exciting, alive. She thirsts for his companionship, for communication with him, for nearness to his person. It is with near-impatience that she dreams of him, and talks about him with the young women of the court. No one who interacts with her is left with any doubt that she is straining at the leash for him—wistfully available but never overly aggressive.

SELF-PERSPECTIVE: Lest we think this woman is merely a young ingenue, infatuated with the pomp and prestige of the sovereign, she gives us insight into her introspection. Being a realist, she knows that all who see her will conclude she was not "to the manor born." Her skin is tanned, indicating that she has worked in the fields. She was not born with a silver spoon in her mouth.

She freely admits that her brothers have not pampered her; she has not learned to live the life of leisure. She has family problems, and she knows that many other women in the court view her with jealousy. Still, her love for the king vaults all these barriers, and with a disarming simplicity she continues to sharpen her affection for him.

INITIATIVE: The flocks must be tended and the vineyards cared for. Life must go on, but how much sweeter it is when the one you love continues to insert himself into your activities. Solomon and his bride move independently to be together and to show love to one another. There is no passivity on the part of either; each exerts him or herself for the object of the heart. Each is sure of him or herself with the other, knowing the welcome is always there, but approaching with courtesy and consideration, with respect and trust.

LEADERSHIP: Surrounding all the romantic verbiage of the poem is a halo of honor for the position of the groom. He is clearly the partner with primacy. I do not believe this is purely Syrian culture reflecting from the pages of the Song. Rather, it is reflective of the implicit husband-wife function. The king accords to his lover appropriate rank, dignity, and esteem, but he is the king, the ruler.

Such a relationship is natural, secure, and liberating for the Shunamite woman. Within the boundaries of her marriage, she can fulfill her highest expectations and develop her best potential. The more she adores him, the greater is his adoration and willingness to enrich the relationship. His own accomplishments soar with the knowledge that the one he loves supremely endorses him and enhances him.

PERMANENCE OF RELATIONSHIP: Setting this love apart from all other loves is the understanding that it is forever. It is no delirious fantasy; it is a flesh-and-blood, real-life avowal of commitment. God never intended for men and women to come together in a temporary romantic liaison, only to be torn apart with bleeding hearts because of infidelity. "What therefore God has joined together, let no man separate" (Matt. 19:6), said our Lord. The words of the bride are poignant: "Put me like a seal over your heart, like a seal on your arm. For love is as strong as death. . . . Many waters cannot quench love, nor will rivers overflow it . . ." (Song 8:6, 7).It may be well to note here the following commentary on these verses:

> King Solomon, who composed this Song under the inspiration of the Holy Spirit, here transcends his own practices, for his granting the wish of the Shulamite would have ruled out his polygamy. This expression of fervent and irresistible love from the lips of the bride points to the monogamous character of marriage. Marriage is the union in love of one man and one woman and any intrusion by a third party violates the unique relationship between the two. The desire of one who truly loves is so strong that he gives himself completely to the other. . . . Not even Solomon with all his wealth could

buy the love of the Shulamite girl. Instead, she gave it to him spontaneously and her love was overwhelmingly great. (from *The Wycliffe Bible Commentary*, p. 603.)

Solomon's Selection of a Wife

A self-determined purity, a choice of chastity, sets this woman apart from others. She has a single eye for her one lover. Call it innocence, naiveté, but it wins for her the heart of the king, singled out from all the others for his exclusive love and attention.

I cannot help but connect Paul's words to the Philippians:

Whatever is true, whatever is honorable, whatever is right, whatever is pure, whatever is lovely, whatever is of good repute, if there is any excellence and if anything worthy of praise, let your mind dwell on these things (Phil. 4:8).

The marriage relationship is no place for ugliness or dramatic show. God desires that husband and wife live romantically, lovingly, shielding their personal inside relationship from the harsh intrusions of selfish whims. Granted, the Song is an ideal picture, but God never shows us fantasy—this kind of love is within the reach of every woman. Look at the Shulamite. Do you fit into her sandals?

Well, I would like to walk in her shoes, you say, but when I try them on, I need a good shoehorn—I'm not even sure they fit. And what about this physical closeness? How did she know she would buy his brand of lovemaking?

Plenty of women worry about what's normal in lovemaking and what's perverted. But the sex technique books have a ready answer: just about anything falls into the 'normal' category, thus catching women between the devil and the deep. No woman wants to be called narrow and prudish, but neither does she want to be sexually exploited.[2]

We who are schooled in the democratic process find the concept of submission hard to swallow. We assume, even in lovemaking, a fifty-fifty agreement. But the fluidity of love will sometimes call for a ninety-ten proportion, or even one hundred-zero. At one point in the Song the king says, "Do not arouse or awaken my love, until she pleases" (Song 8:4). Patience and forbearance is exercised in her favor. Real love never exploits. True love will always do what is best for the other one; it will read between the lines and give the benefit of the doubt consistently.

What of estrangement? In a social group recently we were discussing the plight of singles who are alone at holiday seasons. One woman seemed to be revealing an inside wound as she said, "Yes, but there is something worse: being together with someone who isn't really with you—that's *real* loneliness."

Dr. Otto Sperling points out the vastness of this problem:

The frustration of loneliness is a tragedy of such magnitude that it eclipses other frustrations completely. Like cancer, it is a scourge of the modern age, and its devastating domain is not only the geriatric ward, where the problem is serious enough. It is awful beyond description for the lover to be rejected by the beloved. . . .[3]

Rejection will not grow where lovers work at giving themselves to each other.

In her perceptive essay, "Loneliness . . . An American Malady," Carson McCuller observes: ". . . after the

first establishment of identity there comes the imperative need to lose this new-found sense of separateness
and to belong to something larger and more powerful
than the weak, lonely self." Marriage, including the
love relationship it affords, is God's greatest provision
for belonging. But it must be handled with care, with
feeling. Someone has said we no longer question man's
ability to think as much as we doubt his ability to feel.

The Song of Solomon is about feeling. God has spoken to our center of emotions. He desires that our heads
find expression through our hearts.

Study Questions: Chapter 5

The quality of love in Solomon's Song far excels the "average" marriage relationship. The bride proclaims:

He has brought me to his banquet hall, and his banner over me is love. (2:4)

The New Testament echo is found in Eph. 5:25,31 and Titus 2:4. Discuss this biblical concept of love. What does this kind of love look like in twentieth-century marriage?

6

Esther: Beauty and the Best

As the world has slowly sifted through the charred remains of World War II, it has come upon a glistening jewel—a woman named Cornelia ten Boom. Corrie was past fifty years of age when German soldiers, under orders from the Nazi High Command, invaded her home town of Haarlem in the Netherlands in February, 1944. With some thirty-five members of her family and friends, she was forced from a sickbed and arrested for concealing and befriending Jews who were trying to escape Hitler's racial purge.

"That night," wrote Corrie, "God used Father to prepare each of us in a special way for the unknown times that lay ahead." Her father was the beloved "grand old man of Haarlem," a respected, highly competent, and God-fearing watchmaker. "Father asked my brother Willem to read Psalm 91 and then Father prayed."[1]

He that dwelleth in the secret place of the most High shall abide under the shadow of the Almighty. I will say of the Lord, He is my refuge and my fortress: my God, in him

will I trust. Surely he shall deliver thee from the snare of
the fowler, and from the noisome pestilence. He shall
cover thee with his feathers, and under his wings shalt
thou trust: his truth shall be thy shield and buckler (Ps.
91:1-4, KJV).

From the local Dutch police station, through a series
of imprisonments, and climaxing at the dreaded
Ravensbruck concentration camp north of Berlin, Corrie moved in a human nightmare. But she was always
protected in a spiritual cloak provided by Jesus Christ,
which kept her mind and spirit intact. Although today
she has passed her eightieth birthday, her message that
"Christ is Victor!" resounds throughout the world.

It was during another time and in another century
when Jews were suffering under the heels of another
would-be exterminator, that another woman, because
of her valiant faith in Jehovah, stood out clearly from all
others of her time to show the world that "Faith is the
victory!"

The Stage Setting

The centuries prior to the birth of Jesus Christ had
dwindled to less than five when the great Persian
monarch Xerxes, one of the most illustrious of the ancient world, held a mammoth six-month-long feast to
celebrate his intended military sweep against Greece.
Selling this campaign to his political and military chief-
tains was critical, inasmuch as his father had attempted
a similar expedition unsuccessfully.

In the opening verse of the book of Esther, splendor
and power surface. Xerxes, called by his title,
Ahasuerus, reigned from India (the Indus Valley which
is now known as West Pakistan) to Ethiopia. Residing
in this widespread dominion were large numbers of

captive Israelites who had been displaced under the Babylonian captivity. Some had been allowed to return to Jerusalem under their leader, Zerubbabel, to begin rebuilding the temple. Others remained.

Xerxes was living at his winter residence at Susa, two hundred miles east of Babylon, one of several Persian capitals, when the celebration of the intended offensive was held. The magnificence of the palace decor can be envisioned by the biblical description. The court of the garden, focus of the climactic seven-day banquet which was open to the public, was draped in violet and white linens. These tapestries, hung between marble columns, were held in place by cords of fine purple linen and silver rings. The furniture consisted of couches of gold and silver on a dazzling floor of marble, mother-of-pearl, and precious stones. Drinks were served in gold containers—everyone could have as much as he wanted.

On the final day of the lavish feast, the king sent seven chamberlains to bring beautiful Queen Vashti to him for display. He was saturated with alcoholic drink; nevertheless, his word was law.

Absolute dictators of modern times have no edge on the ancient monarchs. So feared and honored were they that only a few chosen slaves and select advisers were ever allowed even to see their faces. Power was derived from a mixture of royal bloodlines and military prowess, overlaid with a terrifying facade of religious intimidation. Of Xerxes' father, Darius I, one historian has written:

> He fought his way to the throne room over the bodies of those who opposed his right to rule. These men who wore the purple by virtue of the sword, rather than by the legality of inheritance, often mounted propaganda campaigns to legitimatize their rule, to convince the people

that they reigned by a right at least as great as that of
lineage . . . to convince all men that only he was the
chosen of gods and history to direct the destiny of the
empire.[2]

Whether possible shame and humiliation was involved for Vashti we do not know, but she refused to
come and a public divorce was proclaimed. Undoubtedly she knew disobedience meant death, but in an
almost contemporary type of display of women's
rights, she rebuffed the king and could have sparked a
rash of marital defiance in the homes of the people. So
reasoned the royal advisers. Accordingly, a law stating
"that all the wives shall give to their husbands honor"
was passed and the word dispatched throughout the
empire. The wives were "put in their places."

> . . . when the king's edict . . . is heard throughout all his
> kingdom, great as it is, then all women will give honor to
> their husbands, great and small. And this word pleased
> the king . . . So he sent letters . . . that every man should
> be master in his own house . . . (Esther 1:20-22).

Fitting in perfectly with Xerxes' frame of mind, a
beauty contest was contrived to search out the fairest
specimen of womanhood to be the new queen.

Enter Esther

Mordecai was a Benjaminite living in Susa. He was
the guardian of his uncle's orphaned daughter, Hadas-
sah. His young cousin had assumed the Persian name
Esther, meaning "a star."

If Esther ever had a quiet question about what she
would do with her life, it was soundly resolved by a
two-pronged answer: tradition and circumstance! Her
home training unquestionably cast her in the mold of a
proud Jewess, unwilling—virtually unable—to bow to

the corrupt and immoral gods of Babylon. Her future seemed to hang—together with that of her displaced people—in the greedy balance of Persian domination and eventual extinction.

But once again God intervened in a dark moment of history to show His power, to vindicate the words of Isaiah to Cyrus: "That men may know from the rising to the setting of the sun that there is no one besides Me. I am the Lord, and there is no other" (Isa. 45:6).

The Beauty Contest

Mordecai had a wild idea. Why not place beautiful Esther in the competition? He did, and in contrast with the other contestants, she quickly revealed her remarkable upbringing. Her natural facial and bodily beauty had been well preserved. Her personality was attractive and magnetic. No one detected that she was a Jewess and Mordecai advised her to be silent on this matter.

From the modern viewpoint, preparation of ancient would-be queens is fascinating. A retinue of maids gave the prospect proper diet and grooming. A whole year of preparation was required to go before the king. The beautification process consisted of a six-month regimen with oil of myrrh followed by six months of spices and other cosmetics.

Myrrh is a gum resin from a tree-shrub which grows in parts of northern Africa. The fruit is smooth, somewhat larger than an English pea, colored variously from a reddish-yellow to brown or red. The taste is bitter. Myrrh was used by the Israelite priests for holy anointing oil, for embalming (It was used on the body of Christ.), and as a drug when mixed with other herbs. Its use in the book of Esther was for purification. It was an antiseptic, an astringent, and a stimulant. For a woman to have close bodily contact with the monarch, she obviously had to be free of any disease or malodor.

The second half of the make-ready included a variety of perfumes. Perhaps it was a kind of trial and error with various mixtures, but a series of beauty treatments was given. At the time of her appearance before the king, the candidate could also receive jewelry to wear or other adornment. She was allowed to look her very best.

Esther astounded everyone by asking for nothing extra. She went before the king with, in the words of Peter, the ornament of "a gentle and quiet spirit."

The result was dramatic; the king loved her and set the royal crown on her head. It is intriguing to note "she found favor and kindness." These men in power were not known for benevolence to anyone.

The Weight of the Crown

The new queen must have known that the future of her race hung in the balance. She was counseled to conceal her identity, which seems to show it was dangerous to be identified with Yahweh, the God of the Israelites. Whether Mordecai planned in advance to assault the throne through his cousin is not clear, but the idea that one alien subject could make a dent in an enormous bureaucratic Persian court is ridiculous. In fact, a whole debate could be waged over the situational ethics involved. Yet God allowed a miracle to be lived out.

No sensational phenomenon struck the court when Esther ascended the throne. As often happens in the lives of God's children, the simple ebb and flow of men's affairs are used by Him to move His person into a strategic position. Not only had Esther's physical and temperamental loveliness propelled her far ahead of the competition, she went on to show that she was mentally tough enough for a position of responsibility.

Without question, God directs some women to step out of the home and family circle to assume a role of broader management. The "working woman," as we call her, shoulders heavy stewardship. Esther demonstrated her capability to perform with distinction.

The villian, Haman, rose to the forefront of activity in God's flawless timing. Vying for prestige and power, he was promoted to a kind of "big man on campus." The king "advanced him and established his authority over all the princes who were with him" (Esther 3:1). Everybody bowed down and paid homage to him—everyone except Mordecai. As guardian of Esther, who was now close to the seat of power, Mordecai found this an impossible predicament.

Haman was descended from Agag, the infamous king of the Amelekites. The story of Saul's disobedience to God is told in 1 Samuel; he defeated this enemy but captured the king along with the choicest animals. On this occasion the Lord said to Samuel: "I regret that I have made Saul king . . ." (1 Sam. 15:11).

He disobeyed, he lied, and from the prophet Samuel he received the stinging rebuke: ". . . to obey is better than sacrifice, and to heed than the fat of rams" (1 Sam. 15:22).

To Mordecai, Haman was intolerable. It was unthinkable that he, a proud son of Benjamin, should ever bow in deference to this uncircumcized Gentile. Such insubordination obviously set off a rage in Haman. He knew the Jewish heritage; to attack Mordecai openly would be illegal and unwise. His method would have to be underhanded.

Appearing before Ahasuerus, Haman convinced the ruler that there was a group of lawless people who should be removed. He even offered to pay well from his own pocket into the royal treasury to have something done about the matter. His apparent loyalty and concern moved the monarch so much that he gave Haman his signet ring, sign of complete authority to do as he pleased.

> And letters were sent by couriers to all the king's provinces to destroy, to kill, and to annihilate all the Jews, both young and old, women and children, in one day . . . and to seize their possessions as plunder . . . The couriers went out impelled by the king's command while the decree was issued in Susa the capital; and while the king and Haman sat down to drink, the city of Susa was in confusion (Esther 3:13,15).

In order that the news would reach everyone simultaneously, Haman utilized the very efficient Persian postal system. His announcement set off a plague of despair. Mordecai's response was that of any stricken Jew: he put on sackcloth and ashes—mourning. What else? Other Jews joined in fasting, weeping, and wailing.

Esther was notified of her cousin's mourning, but apparently did not understand the reason for it. In consternation she tried to send garments to him in order that he might come and talk with her. She could have no contact with anyone in sackcloth and he was not allowed to advance past the palace gate. Her representative, however, brought back the bad news, and with it Mordecai's plea that she intercede for her people before the king.

Such a suggestion posed another impasse. Her reply:

> All the king's servants and the people of the king's provinces know [that is, "everybody knows"] that for any man or woman who comes to the king to the inner court who is not summoned, he has but one law, that he be put

to death, unless the king holds out to him the golden scepter so that he may live. And I have not been summoned . . . (Esther 4:11).

His answer:

Do not imagine that you in the king's palace can escape any more than all the Jews. For if you remain silent at this time . . . you and your father's house will perish. And who knows whether you have not attained royalty for such a time as this (Esther 4:13–14)?

The monkey was clearly on Esther's back. The climactic moment of her life had arrived and with it a very dangerous decision.

I am reminded again of *The Hiding Place* and the fateful decision dear Mr. ten Boom made when he was asked, "Would you be willing to take a Jewish mother and her baby into your home?"

Father held the baby close, his white beard brushing its cheek, looking into the little face with eyes as blue and innocent as the baby's . . . 'You say we could lose our lives for this child. I would consider that the greatest honor that could come to my family.'[3]

Queen Esther had no way of knowing that at this juncture history was focused upon her. One can only imagine the storm of rage which must have swept her as she read the edict and comprehended Haman's fiendish scheme. Her role became clear and she issued a request for all her people in Susa to fast for three days. ". . . And I will go in to the king, which is not according to the law; and if I perish, I perish" (Esther 4:16)

Weaving the Handwork of History

"What is troubling you, Queen Esther? And what is your request? Even to half of the kingdom it will be given to you" (Esther 5:3).

Ashasuerus had extended the golden scepter and received his queen. The action was unprecedented and I am sure her heart was pounding. ". . . may the king and Haman come this day to the banquet that I have prepared for him . . ." (Esther 5:4).

This seems to be an invitation on short notice—a kind of spur-of-the-moment luncheon date. The record shows that the king "quickly" found Haman, and the two were entertained by the Queen. As they drank their wine, Esther felt the need for more time and asked them to return for another banquet "tomorrow."

Haman was delighted. Although he was upset to see Mordecai as he left the palace, he went home and hastily organized a testimonial dinner for himself. To his wife, Zeresh, and his friends, he recounted how he had climbed the ladder of success. Clearly things were going his way. Imagine! Me! Having dinner with the king and queen! How exclusive can you get!

One little loose thread remained to mar an otherwise perfect set-up—Mordecai. He was always there at the gate. When everybody else bowed down to Haman, who was next-in-command to the king, this Jew stood upright, staring insolently. You can almost hear him describing the scene in his sitting room full of worshipful friends and family.

Why get uptight over one mere rebel? Build a gallows, suggested Zeresh in a plot reminiscent of Jezebel's. (See 1 Kings 21.) Have Mordecai hanged in the morning. He will be out of the way and you can enjoy the banquet in the evening.

Haman probably slept well that night. The conspiracy was working like a charm and he would be ready with his stinger for Mordecai at daybreak. But Xerxes had insomnia. He decided to catch up on his official reading and called for the chronicles and records of the court. As they were being read, a very interesting item popped up: two doorkeepers had surreptitiously tried to plan his assassination, but the murder was thwarted by a loyal subject named Mordecai.

Hmm-mm, wait a minute. "What honor or dignity has been betstowed on Mordecai for this?" he asked. Such outstanding valor should be rewarded.

"Nothing has been done for him," his servant responded.

So the next morning the king called in Haman, who had just arrived to discuss his hanging plan. Bursting with his unfinished business, the king started in, "What is to be done for the man whom the king desires to honor?"

Exploding with ego, Haman immediately assumed that he himself was the honored one, and so he made an ostentatious suggestion: "Let them bring a royal robe which the king has worn, and the horse on which the king has ridden, and on whose head a royal crown has been placed . . ." (Esther 6:8). And he proceeded to outline a lengthy and impressive ceremony in the city square.

"Take quickly the robes and the horse as you have said, and do so for Mordecai the Jew, who is sitting at the king's gate; do not fall short in anything of all that you have said" (Esther 6:10).

What a turnabout! These words of the king probably left Haman speechless and shocked, but the plan by royal fiat was carried out. This time it was Haman who covered his head in mourning. He rushed home to tell his family the disturbing news, but instead of bolstering him, they added to his fears. Zeresh chose this moment to share some backyard gossip about this Jewish Jehovah. "If Mordecai, before whom you have begun to fall, is of Jewish origin, you will not overcome him, but will surely fall before him."

Now, there was a supportive wife! Now it was *his* turn to have a pounding heart! Interrupting the huddled family council, the chauffered limousine arrived for Esther's banquet. Haman's whole device had boomeranged; he had no appetite.

Queen Esther had mastered the Persian court etiquette and hers was no small dinner party. It was a truly oriental banquet of long duration. So it was the second day that her actual request was verbalized to the king. Her words, her timing, her self-control—all was scheduled and in order.

> If I have found favor in your sight, O king, and if it please the king, let my life be given me as my petition, and my people as my request; for we have been sold, I and my people, to be destroyed, to be killed and to be annihilated. Now if we had only been sold as slaves, men and women, I would have remained silent, for the trouble would not be commensurate with the annoyance to the king, (Esther 7:3–4).

It is, she was saying, only because there is mass murder at hand that I bother you with this matter.

Such electrifying news could evoke only one question: Who? The code of Hammurabi, on which the law of the Medes and Persians was built, could tolerate what some might call injustices, but it did not countenance genocide.

The moment of truth was chiming on Haman's clock. He could not hide any longer. "A foe and an enemy is this wicked Haman!" Esther's beautiful dark eyes must have flashed with incriminating fire. The record says simply that Haman became terrified.

As Esther's accusation sank into the king's understanding, it was translated into anger. Ahasuerus rose from his place and took a walk in the garden. He was suddenly befuddled. An old family skeleton had been yanked out of the closet and he needed some fresh air to clear his mind.

Again history throws an interesting sidelight on the biblical record. Haman was clearly making a power play; was he, indeed, aiming for the throne itself? Apparently the same thing had happened to Xerxes' father, Darius.

In his "inaugural" statement unearthed by archaeologists, Darius first established his bloodline for five generations back to make his point that royal blood ran in his veins. His second claim was made by sanction: Ahura Mazda, god of the Persians, gave him the kingdom to rule. Another man, he told his people, a man claiming to be the son of Cyrus the Great, had already laid claim to the throne. Not true, he declared; someone bearing a close resemblance had fomented a revolt, throwing the realm into chaos. To restore tranquility, the impostor had fallen to Darius' sword.

Whether this is simply a curious tale, or a 2,500-year-old Watergate, we cannot know. At any rate, Xerxes was suffering the chronic problem of an emperor—holding on to the reins of power.

Meanwhile, Haman had fallen down next to Esther, begging for his life. When the king returned and saw him in this posture, his suspicions flared: "Will he even assault the queen with me in the house?" The very words from the royal mouth condemned Haman and before Ahasuerus was through speaking, the servants had covered his face (i.e., placed a hood over his head, the customary preparation for execution). They quickly revealed the news that had not yet reached the king: "Behold indeed, the gallows standing at Haman's house fifty cubits high [75 feet], which Haman made for Mordecai who spoke good on behalf of the king!" (Esther 7:9).

"Hang him on it." The sentence was swift and brief.

Esther casts a long shadow into the twentieth century. What does she tell me as a woman? Let me suggest seven directional signs from this page out of God's history book.

1. *Be assured that God has put you where you are and that His timing is right.* The book of Esther provides a reference point of faith, a confirmation that God is in control, that He puts the right people in the right places at the right time. The circumstances may have seemed trivial, but the destiny of the Jewish people was at stake. Our own destiny as Americans was affected by a seemingly trivial decision of Christopher Columbus.

In his fascinating biography of Columbus, *Admiral of the Ocean Sea,* Samuel Eliot Morison describes those last agonizing days before Queen Isabella's three ships sighted land on their exploratory voyage to the new world: ". . . great flocks of birds were passing overhead to the southwestward."[4]

Remembering that the famed Portuguese explorers had used the migrations of birds for their own reckonings, he followed them.

> This judgment was good, for the fall migration of North American birds to the West Indies via Bermuda was in full flight, and Columbus' decision to follow these feathered pilots rather than his inaccurate manmade chart was vital for the whole future of Spanish colonization.[5]

Columbus was, in fact, a man of strong personal faith in God. "His serenity came from an inward assurance and confidence in God, not from superior knowledge," wrote Morison. At the same time, he cites proof that he was a superb seaman, that he had what a great French seaman called *le sens marin*, that intangible and unteachable God-given gift of knowing how to direct and plot "the way of a ship in the midst of the sea."[6]

Esther and Mordecai, displaced Jews living in an alien land, possessed a spiritual *le sens marin*, which God used to accomplish His purpose.

2. *Take care of your body.* It is the most precious material possession you have. On her tape, entitled, "God's Beauty Contest," Irma Warr of Oklahoma City says God prepares each daughter not only to enter, but to win His beauty contest. Does everybody know you're royalty, she asks? Maybe you've decided you are an ugly duckling, or a tomboy, or too spiritual for that. Or perhaps you have bought the line that you must do your own thing. This may be a coverup, says Mrs. Warr; the girl who lacks inwardly sometimes overdoes the outside. God does the interior decorating and we are responsible before the world to be outwardly attractive as well. From Esther we can learn that God blesses, honors, and uses physical beauty, health, and wholeness. Grooming and care bring glory to the One who made our bodies.

3. *Submit to godly home training and parental authority.* As Esther went into that palace to live, she took with her an internal textbook. All the early training from her wise cousin was indelibly written in her mind and heart. She did not put it on and off like a piece of clothing; her involuntary responses made her queenly. She had, no doubt, been submissive to her foster father, served him in the home, and learned obedience to authority. Such training was the best preparation

she could have for a position of leadership and public example.

4. *Be a loyal citizen of the government*. Mordecai and Esther operated totally within the framework of their alien culture. They demonstrated that it is possible. On only one occasion did Mordecai disobey—at the point where the local law conflicted with the first commandment. He *could not* bow down to Haman. But he had faithfully intervened to save the life of an ungodly ruler. Is it possible that we often shy away from the secular scene because it is too hard to live under its regimen? God is sovereign; His grace is sufficient. Yes, it is possible.

5. *Brains must accompany beauty*. Use your head if you want to keep it. Moving out of the domestic surroundings, away from the home of cousin Mordecai, and into the palace must have been painful and frightening for Esther. She was close to the seat of power and also of personal peril. She had to have her wits about her. There was much to learn and the world looks more threatening from the palace window. With all of our current opportunity for education and self-development, it seems to me that God is saying to us women today: Think! "Be diligent to present yourself approved unto God . . ." (2 Tim. 2:15). We have no excuse for ignorance.

6. *God has no restrictions on women aiming for the top in any field of endeavor*. Just be sure your motives are right. Whether God privileges me to be a wife with a primary responsibility to one man, or as a single woman with a generalized "help-meet mandate," I must assume my job with courage.

Esther's vocation—sharing a throne—is instructive to the modern professional woman. Moving into the

world of commerce, of business, of politics—
whatever—is to face culture shock. Like living in a
strange land, it presents a gigantic challenge.

The islands of the Pacific sparkle with unique
beauty. Bleached sand rises out of transparent blue
water. As if to tack them in place, graceful palm trees
spike these floating scraps of paradise. Volcanic rock
holds them down like so many oversized paper
weights. If I were to drop down and float ashore on the
lacy fringe of a roller coaster wave, the trade winds
would blow my hair dry and the sun would dry my
clothes. I would even find the people appealing.

A stranger in their midst, I would probably be confronted with a challenge: Was this song of welcome
which they sang a threat to life and limb? I would need
to understand: Did they intend to host me or roast me?
At first it might be a very uncertain feeling. Similarly,
going "to work" in a business or profession produces
severe culture shock for many young women.

Esther took a grave risk; yet that risk helped define
the power of God. It elevated her to a new respect
before her people. The Feast of Purim, remembered to
this day by the Jews, commemorates her courage and
God's deliverance.

The woman to whom God entrusts influence over
other people must take risks. For Esther, adjustment to
court life meant a switch from a passive existence as a
subservient daughter to Mordecai to an active, initia-
tory lifestyle. She was limited by a strong, male-
oriented society, and she faced a sinister foe. Yet with
fearlessness she faced her problems because she had
already made the basic decision: Serve Jehovah at any
cost. The rest was relatively simple; she did not act
without serious thought and obvious apprehension,
but she acted in faith. God always honors the bravery
of faith.

Study Questions: Chapter 6

1. What are some sacrifices a godly woman executive must make?

2. If God gifts a woman with leadership, and opens the doors for her to perform in that capacity, how should she relate to the men under her jurisdiction?

7

Mary: Vessel Unto Honor

A church in Dallas wished to dramatize for the community what Christmas meant and erected on the front lawn a simple wooden manger filled with hay. It was surrounded by a large square wooden frame wrapped in transparent plastic and tied with a huge red bow. God's Christmas gift to the world: a humble baby.

I drove by this graphic portrayal and thought, how appropriate. Then the next day I drove by again, and in the meantime one of our Texas northers had blown through with its characteristically high winds. The display was in shambles. The wooden frame had cartwheeled off to the side and lay with a broken side and the red bow askew. The manger itself had tilted over and the hay was mostly scattered.

What a picture, I thought, of the treatment the world has given God's Christmas gift. For many, the story of Christ in the manger is simply one more legend to be tossed aside and forgotten. However, the true accounts of Jesus' birth, life, and death also give us insight into the life of Mary, the mother of Jesus. She came into historical view with delicate poignant beauty; she

lived to stand by the cross on which her Son was put to
death in crushing horror.

Mary Was Available

Does it not stir your feminine curiosity to look at
Mary? What kind of a woman did God choose, out of all
the women He could have formed, to be the human
cradle for His own perfect Son?

If we strip away the heavy ornate layers of romantic
imagery and restrict ourselves to biblical record, we
find that only four New Testament writers refer to Mary
by name. These references remind us Christ was born
of a woman; this is to secure His true manhood. But
Mary, the woman Mary, was much like any other devout young Jewish girl. Can we not conclude that God
uses His hand-picked instruments, not for what they
are of themselves, but for what He makes of them?
Mary was available.

Announcement of Good News

Return with me to that fascinating first chapter of
Luke. The angel Gabriel steps into the spotlight with
exciting news. Where was Zacharias on that fateful
day? He was in the temple doing his job. He and his
wife Elizabeth lived every day with hearts that were
open and honest toward God, and the old priest went
faithfully to perform his function as God had commanded long before.

They were living with an unanswered question:
Why no children? Every Jewish home considered children to be a sign of God's blessing. Had not the psalmist said that children are a reward, like arrows in a

man's quiver (Ps. 127)? They had none, yet they continued to worship Him in their autumn years.

The headline news caught Zacharias off guard. "You will have a son." No, it could not be true. He must be hearing things, having hallucinations. Was it because of his age that he could not believe and insisted upon proof from God? Nothing miraculous had happened for so long that Zacharias for some reason felt he had to have a "sign." God gave it to him; he lost his speech!

When the good priest came out to the people, his face told the story without words. Something *really* tremendous had happened—they did not know what, but something. When he got home to Elizabeth he no doubt used sign language to tell her what the angel had said. Suddenly it all became clear why there had been no baby all these years.

Some puzzles of life are never put together on this side of heaven; we go to our graves without answers. God sometimes wants us to believe Him without any visible proof that He has heard our prayers. The eleventh chapter of Hebrews lists many of these gold-star believers who died in this way, without knowing what was on the bottom line. It never added up.

My husband's godly grandmother was one of these. She prayed that her son, graciously spared through military service in Africa, the Middle East, Europe, and Korea, would receive Christ personally. She died without an answer to that prayer. But God answered. He is faithful. Long after Grandmother's death, after forty-two years of my husband's prayers for his father's salvation, Dad Hendricks received the Lord four months before God took him from this earth.

For Elizabeth, the years dropped away. She miraculously conceived in her old age, and I am sure the news set the feminine Jewish grapevine to buzzing.

An Angelic Housecall

With precise timing, Gabriel paid his second call, this time to the humble village of Nazareth. There he appeared to Mary and gave her news very similar to what had been delivered to Zacharias. Elizabeth, he had said, would bear a son whose name would be John. His birth would be with great joy and gladness.

This time he spoke similarly to Mary. His approach underscores the high regard young Jewish women held for this announcement. For hundreds of years they had known that one of them would be singled out for the honor of this special motherhood. At long last the moment had come.

Looking closely at Mary, I see a blend of three cardinal qualities plaited together, as it were, into a model life: stability, sensitivity, and spirituality. All come to the fore when Gabriel speaks to her.

"Hail, favored one! The Lord is with you!" Mary was as startled as any of us would be. Luke's record tells us she tried to think what the angel meant. Her instinctive reaction was to think. She did not react emotionally to this suprise. Rather, she martialed her reasoning power to put it all together. She was asking herself: Why me?

But she also felt emotion. The angel said, "Do not be afraid" because she must have been a little frightened. Who wouldn't have been?

Then the news: ". . . You have found favor with God. And behold, you will conceive in your womb, and bear a Son, and you shall name Him Jesus. He will be great, and will be called the Son of the Most High; and the Lord God will give Him the throne of His father David; and He will reign over the house of Jacob forever; and His kingdom will have no end" (Luke 1:30-33).

That was quite a bombshell to drop on this young lady! There was to be no doubt in her mind; this was not just another baby. It was Jesus, the Greek form of the Hebrew *Joshua*, meaning "Jehovah is salvation." In one short sentence Gabriel outlined the whole future of the world and He was saying, "It's all starting right here with you."

Response to Revelation

What would have been your reaction? She could have said, "Would you please repeat that—I'm not sure I heard you?" Or in unbelief she could have challenged him as did Zacharias: "I just can't believe you're giving me the straight scoop." Or in euphoric immaturity, she could have exclaimed some equivalent of "Whoopee! Wait 'til I tell the girls about this!" Some would see her falling down at Gabriel's feet and lathering them with kisses, mumbling," I am not worthy. Thank you, thank you, thank you!" Or she could have fainted in shock.

Mary's reply lifts the window shade on her remarkably balanced inside self. She was undoubtedly quite young, but she considered herself and her circumstances and asked a most intelligent question: "How can this be, since I am a virgin?" She did not refuse to believe; she simply questioned this biological impossibility.

Gabriel answered clearly: "The Holy Spirit will come upon you and the power of the Most High will overshadow you; and for that reason the holy offspring shall be called the Son of God" (Luke 1:35). God was going to place the fetus within her. Then, as if to show her a sample of God's miracle-working power, Gabriel broke the news of Elizabeth's pregnancy. ". . . she who was called barren is now in her sixth month."

Elizabeth expecting? Dear old cousin Elizabeth? As this overwhelming news hit her, Mary knew the angel was right; "For nothing will be impossible with God." If Elizabeth is having a baby I can believe anything!

"Behold, the bondslave of the Lord; be it done to me according to your word." Not only did Mary believe what Gabriel said, she also indicated her complete willingness to step out into an unknown and extremely threatening situation. The only thing she had to go on was God's Word. Her poise, her courage, and her faith show a young woman of outstanding character and strength. What about Joseph, her fiancé? What about her reputation—getting pregnant out of wedlock? She did not try to make any deal or protect herself in any way. If God wanted her, she was ready right now to give Him everything.

If the narrative would have stopped here, I would have decided Mary was a young lady of extraordinary piety who had probably lived a rather cloistered life, a kind of early-day nun. But the next paragraph profiles Mary as extremely human. She wasted no time in arranging a visit to the hill country to visit her cousin Elizabeth. That's when she got excited. She had to see this with her own eyes. Elizabeth, the one with no children, was a family legend. There had undoubtedly been lots of gossip about her. And now, at her age! Mary got there as fast as she could.

Two Mothers in Conference

With Mary's first word of greeting to Elizabeth, the unborn fetus in Elizabeth's womb "leaped for joy." This movement is interesting physiologically because obstetricians tell us the sense of hearing is the first of the five senses to develop and is quite keen in the unborn child.

Mary, true to the word of the angel, was now overshadowed by the Holy Spirit and even her voice caused this physical reaction. It was apparently a signal to Elizabeth that Mary was the chosen instrument to give birth to our Lord. How the older cousin understood all of this is not explained in the written account, but her words to Mary help to explain how God deals with His people.

"Blessed is she who believed that there would be a fulfillment of what had been spoken to her by the Lord" (Luke 1:45). God puts a high premium upon His Word. In those hours just before the cross when Jesus was praying to the Father, He said, "I have given them Thy Word." This was the message to be delivered—"Thy Word."

Throughout the Bible the emphasis is upon the Word of the Father. What He says to man has always been of critical significance. Those who accept His Word as truth and act upon it are blessed and rewarded. Refusal to believe always brings condemnation. Mary believed and she is commended by Elizabeth.

I once used this story to teach a group of young women how important it is to put everything we are and have on the line for God. Afterward, one of my listeners challenged me: "Well, if I had a shiny angel drop down and speak to me like he did to Mary, it might be a little easier."

I reminded her that we do not know that the angel was shiny—he could have looked like an ordinary man, although Mary obviously knew He was from God. But more than that, we have God's Word in the Bible, a very complete and adequate explanation of all we need to know. ". . . These have been written that you may believe that Jesus is the Christ, the Son of God; and that

believing you may have life in His name," said John
(20:31). It probably was much harder for Mary to believe than for us.

What did she really think? What had happened to her
was overwhelming; how could she absorb it all? There
can be no doubt that Mary was exploding with exhilaration and anticipation, for her thoughts have been
recorded in the inspired poetry called the "Mag-
nificat":

> My soul exalts the Lord,
> And my spirit has rejoiced in God my Savior.
> For he has had regard for the humble state of His
>   bondslave;
> For behold, from this time on all generations will count
>   me blessed.
> For the Mighty One has done great things for me;
> And holy is His name.
> And His mercy is upon generation after generation
> Towards those who fear him.
> He has done mighty deeds with His arm;
> He has scattered those who were proud in the thoughts
>   of their heart.
> He has brought down rulers from their thrones,
> And has exalted those who were humble.
> He has filled the hungry with good things;
> And sent away the rich empty-handed.
> He has given help to Israel His servant,
> In remembrance of His mercy,
> As He spoke to our fathers,
> To Abraham and his offspring forever (Luke 1:46–55).

Looking at these words even from the human standpoint, apart from their inspired nature, it is immediately evident that Mary had a strong relationship
with God. In true Jewish style, she saw her present in
terms of the past history of her people. All her hope was
based upon God's promises to Abraham.

The heritage of her nation was very prominent in her thoughts, especially as they had been downtrodden and deprived. Held captive and despised, the Jews had suffered under the Assyrians, the Babylonians, the Persians, the Greeks, and now the Romans. Mary obviously shared with her kinsmen the many injustices they had known. She herself lived in poverty and for years and years they had lived on hope. Now God had spoken to her personally. She had abundant reason to be overjoyed. She could hardly contain herself.

Luke, the historian and physician, mentions that Mary stayed with Elizabeth three months. Perhaps Mary attended the birth of John the Baptist before she returned to Nazareth. After all, she did need instruction on childbirth. She never imagined she would be giving birth to her baby alone in a stable. The Jews, of course, always had midwives to deliver their babies.

Childbirth was no doubt a familiar procedure to Mary, but she herself had not experienced the process. Now that she was pregnant, having a baby was a different story. It moved out of the realm of the theoretical to the personal. She probably asked Elizabeth every question she could think of and they talked babies day and night during that first trimester of Mary's pregnancy.

Doctors who specialize in the study of newborn babies have confirmed that the first three months of fetal growth are critically determinative. What beautiful provision of God that Mary should be in the company of this older, wiser woman who was fresh from her own early pregnancy. How fitting that those long months of waiting should be spent together!

It was a hallowed moment when the Holy Spirit, with infinite precision of timing, placed that infinitesimal God-sperm into the waiting ovum at the optimum moment of ovulation. That the God of Glory should have been reduced to such tiny size is incomprehensible. That he should have been so very endangered and dependent upon a fragile human woman for sustenance staggers the imagination.

By the third week of fetal life, the Baby had formed a minute head, trunk, and umbilical cord. By the fourth week, there were beginnings of a circulatory system and a rudimentary heart started beating.

After a month, the Embryo had grown to about one-fifth of an inch. Growing at approximately one-fourth inch per week, It measured one-half inch at six weeks. At eight weeks, the Embryo became a Fetus; that is, everything was present that would be found in the full-term Baby. All details must be perfected, all functions exercised. The heart had been beating for a month and the muscles started their first exercises.

It was during Mary's visit in the hill country that she needed to give attention to her diet. Elizabeth would give her good advice. She needed extra sleep, and since she was a guest of her cousin there probably were not as many household chores for her. Perhaps it is safe to assume that Zacharias and Elizabeth were more prosperous than Mary's family, since he was a priest and was provided for. At home she would have had to do heavy work, but here with Elizabeth there was time to rest and to talk. She needed that.

Meanwhile, the blood that was to be shed for the sins of the world was being formed under divine supervision. Until the third month, the Baby had no bone marrow with which to make blood cells. Blood flowed from the placenta through the large umbilical vein carrying oxygen and nourishment before it then ran through the liver tissue. Gradually, however, a main duct formed so that the blood could go rapidly to the heart and be pumped further. As the bone marrow formed, it became the only source for the red blood cells and for a majority of the white cells.[1]

Although Jewish women were very astute in their expertise of pregnancy care, Mary probably knew very little physiology. But God knew. He had obviously chosen a woman with just the right medical history, the perfect blood type, the correct set of genes. She was a properly prepared instrument.

Moment of Incarnation

Into the gentle and joyous mood of a new birth, a harsh political needle is injected, a reminder of the hostile world into which this Child was coming. Emperor Augustus ordered a census. Every so often there would be an imperial command of this sort for purposes of taxation. It meant that every family had to travel to their birthplace where the records were kept. For Joseph, of the royal line of David, it meant a four-or-five-day journey south, from Nazareth to Bethlehem.

Customary transportation for Mary would have been the donkey. Roads, of course, were unpaved. It was certainly a most uncomfortable journey in these last days of her pregnancy. It was "while they were there" that she gave birth. The familiar story tells us that they could not find accommodations in the inn. These commercial establishments were well known for their lack of cleanliness, and so quarters in the stable were probably preferable. There would be clean straw and a water supply and Mary had no doubt brought necessary "swaddling clothes" as was the custom of her day.

Both she and Joseph were probably apprehensive. Were they alone or was there a relative they could call? We do not know. But the Hebrew women handled childbirth well and Mary was mentally and physically prepared.

The labor pains begin—strong contractions. The beautiful head of Christ comes through her open cervix and through the pelvic outlet. The Christ Child is born. Mary wraps Him in the cloth, which holds Him firmly secure and keeps Him dry and warm. There is no separation from His mother; He nurses at her breast. Joseph brings her food. The shepherds come to worship.

What did Mary think? Luke says she "treasured up all these things, pondering them in her heart" (2:19). She had much to think about.

Parental Care

According to Jewish law, male children were circumcised on the eighth day. This particular ceremony may have taken place in Bethlehem, and it was then that He was named *Jesus*.

The law of Moses declared a new mother to be unclean for thirty-three days after the circumcision of her male child. She was to present a sacrifice at the temple and be ceremonially cleansed. The sacrifice was in proportion to the financial ability of the family and Joseph and Mary brought a pair of turtledoves. This offering, indicative of their poverty, was taken to the temple at Jerusalem.

Luke reports that the young parents took Jesus, together with the humble offering, and presented Him to God. It was there that dear old Simeon, "righteous and devout, looking for the consolation of Israel," was prompted by the Holy Spirit to take the Baby into his arms and pray. His eyes had seen "Thy salvation," he said. It is interesting to note that although he was personally looking for salvation for his own race, his prayer ended with the fact that Jesus was "a light of revelation to the Gentiles."

As they witnessed this unusual sight, "His father and mother was amazed at the things which were being said about Him" (Luke 2:33). It would seem Mary and Joseph were so close to their situation, perhaps concerned with the day-to-day necessities of life, that they really could not comprehend the magnitude of their parental mission.

I find their humanity reassuring. They were doing each day what needed to be done and God in heaven was taking care of the big master plan. As a mother, I do not have to worry and fret if I do not understand the major implications of each thing that happens to my children. My job is to obey His commandment: to be faithful in loving and provide as well as I can what each child requires. To know that some day it will all fit together because God has masterminded my whole life is enough and with that He is pleased.

Matthew's gospel account tells the circumstances of Christ's birth from Joseph's standpoint. His tender concern for Mary upon learning of her pregnancy shows clearly the young carpenter must have been a gentle and protective husband and father. He was a competent leader of his home, as well as a skilled wood craftsman.

Some time after the birth of Jesus, Mary and Joseph were still in Bethlehem and apparently had found quarters in a house because this is where the wise men found them. "They came into the house and saw the Child with Mary His mother; and they fell down and worshiped Him; and opening their treasures they presented to Him gifts of gold and frankincense and myrrh" (Matt. 2:11).

There must have been times when Mary looked back and wondered if those things the angel said had all been a dream. But, no, here were the Magi—wise, wealthy men from far away—coming to worship her little Son. It was confirmation that God had spoken.

Again the discordant note of a sinister ruler invades the story. ". . . Arise and take the Child and His mother, and flee to Egypt, and remain there until I tell you. . . ." What must Mary have thought? This time she faced a very long trip across the desert with a small baby. Since they had already been traveling, they were more or less set up for it. They had the donkey, and as out-of-towners it was not suspicious that they should be traveling on. But they did have to travel at night both for safety and probably for escape from the heat of the desert as well.

Back in Bethlehem, many babies ware being murdered by the deranged and sadistic Herod. Again Mary found herself in a strange place and her resourcefulness had to flow freely to make a suitable home for her husband and Child. Again, her strength, stability, and strong faith in God saw her through.

The "all clear" from the angel must have been welcomed gladly. Joseph took Mary and the Child home. They traveled first to Bethlehem, but upon learning that Archelaus had succeeded his father, decided to push on northward, back to Nazareth. There Joseph could ply his carpentry trade. It was a town of many Gentiles, not highly respected by devout Jews, but it offered a place to settle.

Jesus the Boy and His Mother

The early childhood of Jesus is not detailed in the Bible, but a strong bond was most surely formed between Mary and her Son in those early months— possibly years. The scriptural record opens a window at the age of twelve.

Again from Luke's sensitive record, the general temperature of Joseph's home is reported: "And the Child continued to grow and become strong, increasing in wisdom; and the grace of God was upon Him" (Luke 2:40). Undoubtedly He had a brilliant mind. He was extremely keen and strongly oriented toward the prophetic writings and spiritual concerns. Humanly, then, as well as divinely, Jesus was drawn toward the temple.

For the family it was the holiday time, when the long trip to Jerusalem was undertaken with some merriment as the clan made its way to the Holy City for the Feast of the Passover. Children, then as now, chatted and played with cousins and friends from the Nazareth community.

When Jesus did not join his parents on the return trip, they quite naturally assumed He was with some other group in the party. After all, a twelve-year-old boy did not need to stay close to his father. But when night came and He had not yet made His presence known, Joseph became concerned. It was certainly not like his Son to act in this manner. When Joseph inquired, no one had seen Jesus. Can you imagine how Mary must have felt? At first it may have appeared that Jesus was careless, which would be a poor reflection upon His home training. They retraced their steps the next day and began scouring Jerusalem, asking everywhere if they had seen a twelve-year-old boy? Always the answer was no.

Their backtracking took them all the way back to the temple, and there He was—right in the middle of a theological symposium. The doctors of the law, having spent their lives in the study of the Scriptures, were amazed. Not only was He listening to them, but He was asking perceptive questions—brain-twisters, I assume. They had lost all track of time.

Can you see Mary and Joseph, dusty and tired, with

their foreheads in a quizzical frown? They were more dumbfounded than anybody.

Parents, I have observed, have a penchant for wanting their children to be *normal*, not so brilliant that they are "oddballs," and certainly not dull—just pleasantly in between. In recent days we have come to tolerate exceptional brilliance in some sophisticated circles, but ordinary people still want their children to be ordinary. Too much dabbling in high thinking is threatening, and I believe Mary and Joseph may have felt some of this uneasiness. At any rate, they reprimanded Him.

"Son, why have You treated us this way?" That's a normal question from worried parents. The underlying assumption is that Jesus' actions reflected upon them. They did not entertain the thought that there might be another motivation. Obedience to the Heavenly Father, such as He knew it, was outside the realm of their experience and comprehension. Mary spoke for both of them: "Your father and I have been anxiously looking for You."

Any parent who has ever looked for a lost child knows Mary's feeling. She was obviously dismayed when she feared some harm might have come to Him. He might be needing them desperately and they did not know where to look.

We always tend to think of the worst. I remember once going from house to house looking for my younger sister. The tension mounted as we inquired of everyone in the neighborhood. The ultimate question from people was "Have you called the police?" That would have been the last resort in our large city. To have the municipal police patrol car come whizzing down the street and stop in front of our house would have had *everybody* out looking at us. No, not until we just *had* to. Dad finally found her. He used his head and began to think of what she might do and where she might go. Sure enough, she had attached herself to a friendly neighbor lady who was baking cookies.

Jesus' defense of His actions came in the form of a question—very characteristic of the Lord all through His life. "Why is it that you were looking for Me? Did you not know that I had to be in My Father's house?"

Mary, are you possibly guilty of storing away in your heart all those things you knew about your Son and never evaluating them? You have enough facts to know the answer to your question. Think, He is saying. My actions are perfectly legitimate.

Mary and Joseph were as dull as we are. How often do we cry out "why?" without really thinking through what we already know to be true? Again Mary is reported to "treasure all these things in her heart." Her heart is becoming quite a treasure chest and as she grows more mature she will examine the bits and pieces she has collected. One example is the occasion of Jesus' first miracle at Cana.

The Wedding Feast

This gala occasion in Jewish life was at full tilt when it became apparent that the wine supply was gone. Horrors! To run out of wine was the height of embarrassment to a host in that culture. And there was no way to run down to the package store and pick up a bottle; this was social disaster.

Mary may have been acting as hostess, in the same way we would ask a good friend to take charge of a wedding reception. She was apparently there without Joseph; most scholars conclude he died before Jesus began His public ministry. So her natural and instinctive reaction was to consult her Son. What shall we do in this dire predicament? We women appreciate the male's ability to think in a crisis.

Jesus' enigmatic reply jolted her, I am sure. "Woman, what do I have to do with you? My hour has not yet come" (John 2:4). The term "woman" in no way connoted disrespect. It was as if He was seriously explaining she could not take advantage of Him in this public situation. We might paraphrase it, "Mother, I don't think you understand you must not expect Me to help you in a supernatural way here." Of course, He did proceed to perform His first miracle, but Mary needed to understand miracles did not come at her command.

Mary's directions to the servants imply she did understand. "Whatever He says to you, do it," she said. She placed herself in the category of submission to His will. He may or may not have seen fit to perform a miracle, but the decision was His, not hers.

That basic attitude is the key to much of our praying today. We must learn we cannot twist God's arm. Our proper stance is one of willingness to accept what He brings into our lives. Ask? Yes, we are commanded to do that. Believe? Surely, but believe in the Person to whom we pray more than in a specific answer.

Jesus' Family

Mary, like millions of other women, was primarily a wife and mother. She saw herself as a "lowly bondslave" when Gabriel visited her. And although her life had been punctuated with miracles and a close family tie with the incarnate Son of God, it is probable she was mostly occupied with her home, not her firstborn Son. Joseph and Mary went on to have other children. Since it is probable Joseph died while Jesus was still a young man, she was widowed with heavy responsibility for the younger children. We know from the book of Acts that Jesus' brothers most likely did not believe in Him until after His resurrection, and so Mary lived in a home filled with ordinary Jewish children. Undoubtedly she was greatly influenced by them.

Out of this setting, then, Mary and her younger sons came to where Jesus was teaching a large multitude. His reputation for healing and casting out demons had catapulted His name into national prominence. People came from all parts of the land to hear Him teach and there was sharp division over His authenticity. The authorities were at loggerheads over His claim to be God. Rumors and gossip about Him floated everywhere. Some said He was beside Himself. It was through this fog of hearsay that His family made its way to Him—for what reason we do not know. Jesus knew, of course. It would have been inconsistent with His character to be rude to them; we can only speculate their purpose was detrimental to His ministry.

At any rate, they stood at the edge of the large crowd. Mark reports that "a multitude was sitting around Him, and they said to Him. . . ." How can a multitude speak to one person? Apparently, by word of mouth the message was passed along: His mother and brothers want to see Him. Finally, it reached Jesus' ears. Did He know that in unbelief His brothers suspected He was demented and had persuaded His mother to come with them to hide Him away from the public eye? Were they embarrassed by Him? Or perhaps they were concerned that He was working too hard without enough rest and were seeking to whisk Him away for a needed vacation.

Whatever their motive, Mary must have been a part of the plan, but Jesus could not be. Once again, He was about His Father's business. Mary could not know how very short the time was before He would be killed. Perhaps she may have feared for Him because the official opposition had become vocal.

As always, Jesus showed no frustration or hesitancy. He was never caught off guard. His ability to turn any situation into a learning experience was phenomenal. He forced His listeners—and still does—to re-think their old notions. Mother and brothers? Who are they? What is that relationship, really now, He was asking? There is a tie that binds even closer than this blood relationship; it is kinship of spirit. And as He looked at the faces of those seated before Him with open hearts in tune with His, He gestured toward them and called them brothers, sisters, and mothers.

How can that be true? Only the one who has experienced it can truly understand it. It has been my high privilege to work closely with many young Christian people who have come to faith in Christ. Those who are one with us in Him become like part of our families; we are on the same wavelength.

Although the synoptic gospel writers who include this puzzling incident in our Lord's ministry do not record any reaction from Jesus' family, we might wonder if they repeated the words of Luke "They understood not His saying"? I think Mary put it all together as she once again sorted out some of those long-hidden treasures in her heart. She may have felt momentarily rebuffed, but surely she understood eventually. She at least knew what He meant when she finally stood by His cross.

Mary's Strong Spirit

The cross of Christ is, to me, the most moving scene of all the Scriptures. The indignities and humiliation of the torture her Son suffered was enough to have sent an ordinary woman into grief-stricken seclusion. Not Mary. Once again her strength of spirit is evident. She was aged—probably fifty years old, at least. Like a stalwart defender, she stood at the foot of the cross and looked at her precious Son.

She knew Him better than anybody on earth, and she knew how innocent He was. She may have remembered the prophecy of Simeon at the presentation at the temple: " a sword will pierce even your own soul. . . ." Words simply are not adequate to describe how she must have felt to see with her own eyes the battered body of that perfect life she had so carefully and tenderly nurtured. Just to stand there required a fortitude beyond that of most women.

Jesus' Provision for His Mother

And then, in His hour of deepest pain and agony, He looked at her. He knew very well all she had gone through for Him and the sweet willingness with which she had done it. To the very end He was a faithful Son to her as He was to His heavenly Father.

He spoke: "Woman, behold thy son." John was standing close by her. With his own sensitive heart, John surely felt deeply grieved for Mary and Jesus allowed him the privilege of assuming responsibility for Mary in her declining years. There was no mistaking His gracious provision.

He then looked at John. He loved him deeply as a human brother and He said directly to him, "Behold thy mother." John had just the kind of soft, gentle spirit Mary needed.

The last glimpse of this outstanding woman is reported by Luke in the first chapter of Acts. She is listed with the women who gathered in prayer after Jesus' ascension. Her other sons are there too. The family is united in their faith in the One who came to die for their sins and who lived so closely with them.

Mary, the young girl with high hopes for her beauti-

ful baby boy, lived to see Him misunderstood and put
to death by mad powermongers. But she could say,
along with her adopted son, John:

What was from the beginning, what we have heard,
what we have seen with our eyes, what we beheld and
our hands handled, concerning the Word of Life—and
the life was manifested, and we have seen and bear
witness and proclaim to you the eternal life, which was
with the Father and was manifested to us (1 John 1:1–2).

Study Questions: Chapter 7

Mary of Nazareth, wife of Joseph the carpenter, is your assignment as women's editor for the Jerusalem newspaper. Write from the biblical record appropriate news accounts for each of the following:

(1) In the temple with her, after her son had appeared on the file of missing persons (Luke 2:40–52).

(2) At the cross, when her son was being crucified (Luke 23:26–49; John 19:25–30; also cf. Matthew 27, Mark 15).

(3) In Jerusalem with her son's followers, after he had "disappeared" following His widely reported appearance after His death (John 20, 21, Acts 1).

8

Mary and Martha: Tale of Two Sisters

If you have ever had a sister, you can understand Mary and Martha more easily. I had two sisters and when I was growing up, I thought that being in the middle was absolutely the worst place to be. My big sister Dauris had more than three years' running start; it seemed to me she had sewed up all the affections of the family before I got there. If you had asked, I would have told you that the first of everything went to her, that I was an "also-ran."

Sister love is a strange mix of caring and competing. I wanted to do everything Dauris did and trample her in the process. But she developed heart trouble, and slowly our differences paled in the possibility that she might even die. We rode to high school together on the trolley car. I unabashedly carried her books, asked people to stand up so she could sit down, and tended her like a mother hen when she had a fainting spell—all this even though I was extremely shy.

My little sister Anna sprouted up eight years behind me. A cuddly baby was most welcome by then, with us older girls having grown into scrawny, scrapping, mid-sized people. Little Anna was a femme fatale. Whereas we big ones had either light or dark brown hair with nondescript faces and dispositions, she was a captivating brunette with dark eyes and a bubbly personality. She had emerged in the late depression days, undoubtedly straining the family budget. She arrived at the beginning of the war boom, a kind of promise of good things to come.

I remember babysitting one day with Anna during her first year. I told her how much I disliked her and then felt foolish to have said that to a small baby. I recall stealing some money from her piggy bank; I was convinced she got more of everything. Surely I would get caught, giving me a chance to explain how deserving I was, but I never did! A miserable conscience made me finally put it back.

Rudyard Kipling once said: "Never praise a sister to a sister, in hope of your compliments reaching the proper ears."[1] Jealousy is the weed that seems to shoot up in the garden where sisters grow.

The Sisters In Bethany

With personal affinity, then, I stepped into the home of Mary and Martha of Bethany with Dr. Luke and felt quite at home. Here were two sisters who seemed to approximate Dauris and me. Mary and Martha were not two quarrelsome old maids, as some have suggested. This was a normal home where three grown, unmarried children lived together. Lazarus, the brother, was probably the breadwinner, and the two girls kept house. They were most likely about Jesus' age. Remember that all the boy babies two years and under had been killed in this area by Herod. There must have been many unmarried women.

Martha, the older, assumed leadership and prominence. History would have overlooked them, except that the family rose in bold relief as they came in contact with Jesus Christ. He is the One who makes the difference.

In three episodes, Christ used these three apparently ordinary people to make the world stop and take note. The first concerns a routine dinner invitation—if a visit by Jesus could ever be routine—issued to the Galilean teacher. Luke has recorded the action just following the parable of the Good Samaritan, where Christ stressed that what you do for people is more important than what you think about them. Now the reader learns that how we do what we do is even more vital.

The Hostess Who Lost Her Cool

"Martha welcomed Him into her home." How generous of Martha, when you consider an invitation to Jesus surely included his disciples who traveled with Him. Here is a sizeable challenge for any hostess—thirteen men who came to dinner! The house which now stands in the little village of Bethany and which tradition marks as the probable site of this visit would have accommodated this group.

I can visualize the servants washing the dusty feet and hear the hubbub of conversation as the men settled down to await the serving of the food. Like all guests, they undoubtedly looked around at the furnishings, and probably saw a house in apple-pie order. Martha was that kind of woman—no dust on her windowsills.

Someone has said a house should be clean enough to be healthy, but dirty enough to be happy. Martha, however, was a stickler for details and at this moment she was deeply into the kitchen detail. It would be very interesting to know what happened to upset Martha's equilibrium; perhaps one of the servants made a mistake. Whatever it was, she was clearly flustered. She wanted to talk to her sister and get some help from her, but where was Mary? She was with the men, sitting and listening to Jesus!

Martha became furious inside. Imagine! All there was to do and Mary relaxes like a guest! Her frustration level rose quickly. This man Jesus had come across the horizon of this family's life, possibly through the ministry of John the Baptist. John had come through their part of the country on his way into the wilderness, preaching a message of repentance of sin. Thousands had gone out to hear him speak—maybe even this very family. The electrifying charge in John's message had to do with the One who was coming—and He had come. His name was Jesus and He was stirring up a storm. The synagogue leaders loudly denounced Him as heretical. The Roman occupation forces were watching and listening with keen interest.

Very possibly this home had even been one where a pair from the Seventy had lodged. Not long before, Christ had dispatched seventy disciples. They traveled by twos into many of the towns, wherever Christ was planning to teach. It was a learning experience for those men; they had gone out in faith, carrying nothing but the message that the kingdom of God was at hand. Whatever had been the backdrop, the home of Martha and Mary and Lazarus was open to Jesus Christ. He clicked with these three young people and apparently felt very much at ease under their roof.

Martha was a verbal extrovert, an activist. She was a leader. She personified what we today might label the "head-nurse syndrome." As the official hostess, she presented herself in the sitting area and spoke to Jesus Christ. The heat of the cooking may have reddened her face and her voice was high-pitched. She phrased her complaint in the form of a question: "Lord, do You not care that my sister has left me to do all the serving alone? Then tell her to help me" (Luke 10:40).

By focusing the attention on Mary, she hoped to embarrass her sister. But underneath was a rather rude jab at her honored guest. The intent was: "Here I am knocking myself out for You, and You don't even care." She may have even had a tinge of resentment because she herself could not take time to listen to this notable man.

"Do You not care?" Little did Martha realize what an impudent question she had asked. It is reminiscent of the question asked by His disciples in the boat at the height of the storm. "Master, don't you care that we are perishing?" Preposterous! But so very much like us.

The key to Martha's grievance is, or course, herself. ". . . my sister has left me. . . . tell her to help me." Lord, I am the one who is important here—say something so everyone will know.

Frustration is a very real problem. Some years ago I was hostessing a Thanksgiving dinner in our little home, which happened to be short on kitchen counter space. The Lord and I had many conversations about the fact that the house was too small, but He kept saying "wait," and I was doing the best I could—I thought.

Shortly before it was time to serve the meal, I slipped into the hot kitchen to check on my roasting turkey. As I was lifting it from one place to another in a space too tight for efficient operation, it slipped and fell right down on the floor! Two thoughts flashed: (1) the floor's clean and (2) nobody's here. I grabbed it and lifted it to the platter, grateful that no one had witnessed my clumsiness. Suddenly I felt a surge of self-pity. I leaned up against the wall and tears of frustration came to my eyes. In my heart I said, "Lord, I told You so! Now look what's happened! It's all Your fault!"

Then I heard laughter and talking from the other room and I suddenly felt ashamed. What if somebody should come and see me crumpled in such dejection? I grabbed newspaper to put over the mess on the floor and decided I would have it out with the Lord later. I think I know a little of how Martha felt.

Cooling Words from the Lord

Jesus Christ met Martha head-on, with deep love and understanding. Luke quotes Him, ". . . you are worried and bothered. . . . Literally, the text says she was "pulled apart." His response was to the point, characteristic of the Perfect Friend and Counselor. He did not say, "Now Martha, calm down, and relax . . ." as we might have done. Instead, He hit her frontally with gracious insight.

"Martha, Martha"—The double name denotes gentle concern. I am sure His voice alone erased the tension in the air. First, He states the problem: You are worried and bothered about so many things. You're allowing a thousand petty trivialities to fragment you. It's not Mary; it's not me; the problem is *you*. With accurate perception, Jesus Christ handed her a thumbnail sketch of her problem.

How many friends can do that—or would do that? But He not only sketched the problem; he offered a solution. Always Jesus Christ provides the answer.

"One thing is needful. . . ." Here with simple pinpoint focus He makes His message clear—as He did with the rich young ruler who came wanting to know how to obtain eternal life. To him, the Lord said: "One thing is needful. . . ." Paul wrote "one thing I do. . ." We waste time bumbling over priorities. For Martha, and for us as women, here is a well-marked arrow for the direction of our lives. What is it that is needful?

". . . Mary has chosen the good part, which shall not be taken away from her" (Luke 10:42). Mary, "sat," we are told; that is, she settled down at the feet of Jesus. She had chosen the permanent in contrast to Martha's choice of the temporary.

Notice carefully, Jesus did not scold Martha for what she was doing. He understood a hostess was necessary. Her activities were perfectly legitimate, but it was the heart attitude with which she was doing them.

The lesson here is so often obscured. I recall being taught this story in Sunday school as a little child and coming away with the moral to the story: Be like Mary, not like Martha. Kitchen work is bad, servile, lowly, and unspiritual. Nothing could be more erroneous. Martha had a servant heart and the Lord honored that attitude; it was her superficial robe of self-pity which caught His scorn.

Happily, we are not left wondering whether she ever improved. A second episode is presented by the apostle John and the scene is somber. Whereas in Luke healthy people are enjoying a friendly visit, now Lazarus is dying.

When Death Darkens the Door

It has been more than twenty years since I sat in the living room of my parents' home and prayed with Mother that, if it were God's will, Dad would not die. Dad, as I mentioned earlier, was waging a losing battle with an internal cancer and the medical profession had turned in the verdict. "There's nothing more we can do—just a matter of time."

Death's shadow is every bit as real for the child of God as for the unbeliever. We know we have hope beyond the grave, but we are living in the here and now with our emotions and our human needs. The

overwhelming power of death is frightening—
terrifying. The most we often do is to summon those
who care, lean on them to help us stumble through our
grief, and count on time to heal the wound. We are
prone to ask, "Lord, don't You care?"

Mary and Martha knew their brother, Lazarus, was
critically ill. He was apparently a warm, lovable man,
and Jesus had naturally been drawn to his friendship
and his hospitality. Now, as his life seemed to be
ebbing away, the sisters naturally called for their close
family friend, Jesus.

When the word reached the Lord, He said, "This
sickness is not unto death, but for the glory of
God. . . ." Two days went by and He had not begun to
travel. Was He avoiding the heated opposition of the
Jewish leaders down south near Bethany? They had
already tried to stone Him; His disciples advised
against going. Dismissing their precautions, Jesus
headed south, telling them Lazarus had actually died.

When Jesus arrived in Bethany, Lazarus had already
been buried and the two sisters were sorrowing. Although Jesus' coming must have lifted their spirits,
they had obviously already discussed the situation because they both greeted their friend with the same
phrase: "Lord, if You had been here, my brother would
not have died."

They recognized not only Jesus' ability to deal with
death, I believe, but also His indescribable capacity to
feel, to soothe, to calm their own personal storms of
bereavement. Surely they had heard how He raised the
son of the widow of Nain, and how Jairus' daughter
had been restored. Yet they did not dare to suggest He
might do as much for them. Their faith extended only
to prevention—"If You had been here, he would not
have died."

Martha, true to her personality, took the initiative

and went out to meet her arriving friend. The words tumbled out: "If you had been here. . . ." And then she added, "Whatever You ask of God, God will give You." Almost as a hint that she desperately wanted to see a miracle but was afraid to ask.

Jesus' response was simple and clear. "Your brother shall rise again." From her knowledge of theology, Martha decided that surely the Messiah was talking about future events. The language of our Lord was ultra-simple: "I am the resurrection and the life; he who believes in Me shall live even if he dies, and everyone who lives and believes in Me shall never die. [That's dynamite, Martha!] Do you believe this?" (John 11:25,26).

Martha's reply was a prototype of our own. She did not really answer His question. "I have believed that You are the Christ. . . ." Oh yes, Lord, I believe . . . How often have we said it? Lord, I believe You can do anything. But it's a generalized, vague knowledge, instead of a specific belief.

It is interesting that Mary, consonant with her temperament, waited until Martha called her. Her words to the Savior were the same as her sister's: "Lord, if You had been here. . . ." She did not even verbalize her hope for a miracle. She simply wept.

"Jesus wept" (John 11:35). He allowed Himself to feel with Mary, and the perfect Counselor made no attempt to reason, to instruct. He met her where she was. His action was eloquent.

What is the usual response of a man to a woman's crying? "Now, now, stop crying. It won't help. What's done is done. You can't bring him back."

Given His omniscience, it seems Christ could have said, "Now, Mary, I have a plan and it's going to be all right." No, I am sure that in that moment He may have remembered what it was like to lose the one on whom the family depended. It is very possible He sat with His mother beside the body of his earthly father, Joseph, and mourned, realizing He would have to shoulder the heavy burden of supporting the family. He knew personally what the shock of physical death meant.

The scene at the grave is unprecedented. Jesus has taken charge. He is always in command and at this occasion He has moved with grace and courtesy, so that even the casual onlookers remarked about his compassion. Yet they, too, wondered why He could not have prevented the tragedy. It was common knowledge He had healed many sick people. Why did He exclude His good friend Lazarus? Little did they know they were to witness a signal evidence of His deity.

"Take away the stone," Jesus commanded. But Martha, her take-charge instinct flaring up, felt moved to give information and warning—as if our Lord needed her input. Jesus' response is one of understanding and as always, was direct and uniquely fitted for her. Martha, pay attention to Me. What did I tell you? "Did I not say to you, if you believe, you will see the glory of God?" (John 11:42).

Then it happened. A public prayer from Jesus, simply reinforcing for the onlookers what had already happened privately between Jesus and His Father. He was about to perform another miracle, with the intent that "they may believe that Thou didst send Me." Incontrovertible evidence of His deity was coming through their senses—hearing, seeing, smelling, touching—"Lazarus, come forth!"

"Lazarus, come forth." His power over death gleamed before them. John added an intriguing bit of detail: "Many therefore of the Jews, who had come to Mary and beheld what He had done, believed in Him" (John 11:45).

Mary was the one who had sat listening at Jesus' feet.

On this occasion she had fallen at his feet when he approached. Her neighbors and friends knew she deeply believed in Him. It was the combination of her testimony and His miracle that brought saving faith to these onlookers.

What was the response of Mary and Martha? The profound gratitude of their hearts was translated into action in the very next chapter.

An Appreciation Dinner

Life in Bethany took on a new beginning with the resurrection of Lazarus. Can you imagine what a spectacle he must have been, what an object of curiosity, a kind of instant celebrity? But interlacing the exhilaration of Lazarus' return was a somber note of fear for their friend Jesus. The sides were now clearly drawn and there was open talk of putting Jesus to death. Would Jesus, now in seclusion with his disciples, show up for the upcoming Passover Feast in Jerusalem? John tells us that "the chief priests and the Pharisees had given orders that if any one knew where He was, he should report it, that they might seize Him" (John 11:57). Jesus Christ was hunted like a criminal.

It was six days before the Passover when Jesus came to Bethany. Everyone seemed tense over His controversial status, but Christ Himself showed no fear. He came to see His old friends and it was appropriate that a dinner should be given in his honor. It was held at the home of Simon the leper. Two living testimonies to His compassionate ministry—Lazarus, who was raised from the dead, and Simon, who was healed of leprosy—now fearlessly teamed together in the face of official reprimand to honor Him with a dinner of gratitude.

"Martha served." That little detail is significant. *Of*

course Martha served. She was the best in town. When you wanted to have a really well-served meal, you asked Martha—experienced, capable, and another testimony of Christ's ministry. She had come a long way since that first fiery encounter when she complained to the Master. As if to prove Jesus had not condemned her activity, she was found serving with distinction at a function where our Lord was honored by those who loved Him and desired to give their best to Him.

What of Mary? Her intuitive nature told her the end was near. The enemy forces were closing in. Christ Himself had foretold His death and she wished to show Him her grateful heart. She took a "pound of very costly genuine spikenard." This was the Greek litra which equaled ten and one-third ounces. It was a costly perfume which well could have been her share of the family wealth. It was customary in those days to keep such treasures much the same way we would lay aside savings or insurance.

At any rate, she unhesitatingly brought it to the feast in an alabaster jar. While the Lord was eating, she poured it on His head, a gesture of honor, and then wiped his feet with her hair, an act of humility. Mary was always found at Jesus feet. Her overflowing love and appreciation are symbolized as her hair touches his feet in this sacrifice of the most precious possession she had.

Her actions precipitated two contrasting comments. Judas, whose consuming passion in life was money, converted her conduct immediately to the cash equivalent. "It's worth three hundred denarii." This is like throwing money away, he said, obviously not comprehending Mary's motives at all.

It was true, of course. The spikenard was worth almost a year's wages. Poor people did not usually act so recklessly. Why, he asked, did she not use it for charity? That would certainly be the acceptable thing to do, but John editorializes as he informs his readers this comment was merely a cover for Judas' greed. He could not care less for the poor.

"Let her alone, in order that she may keep it for the day of My burial," Jesus said. Judas, you don't begin to understand the impact of this. I am going to die. She understands that and I understand her. What a strange sight all of this must have been to those who stood and watched Jesus being anointed by Mary. Many of them believed on Him.

Friendship with Jesus—just humanly—raised Mary and Martha to new heights. Their own relationship was improved, I am sure, because they shared a common love for Him. The return of their brother from death and disease encouraged them, erasing financial uncertainty. They saw many in their community trust Christ and become new people with a vital spiritual dimension.

Mary was transformed from a receiver to a giver. Back in the book of Luke we see their home known as Martha's place. In John's account, the whole town is known because of Mary. Her vibrant personality has blossomed and reached out to many of her neighbors.

Martha learned to serve with grace. Whereas before she had been calculating and self-pitying, now she was openhearted and generous. They were still the same people, but in Christ they handled their personhood with a gentle confidence which only Jesus Christ can make possible.

Study Questions: Chapter 8

1. What force does Luke's record of 10:37–42 have for the reader, keeping in mind that it is sandwiched in between the Good Samaritan account and the teaching concerning prayer?

2. The raising of Lazarus has far-reaching implications apart from Jesus' personal ministry to the two sisters. What did this incident say to (a) the people of Bethany, (b) the twelve disciples, (c) the chief priests and Pharisees (John 11:47), (d) non-Jews (John 12:19–21)?

9
A Woman For All Seasons

Do you remember Aesop's fable, "The Dog and His Shadow?" A dog was toting a choice morsel of meat back to his lair. As he crossed a bridge, he looked down and saw his reflection in the water. Hunger and greed drove him to drop the meat and to leap into the stream to capture "another" meal. That little caper cost him his dinner. The moral of the story: Beware lest you lose the substance in grasping at the shadow.

Are we American women losing the *substance* of womanhood by grasping at the *shadow?* We are impressed with our shadow. In fact, we are obsessed with our shadow!

For example, every year on the Saturday after Labor Day, an enormous gala is hosted in Atlantic City, New Jersey. Millions of romantically inclined television fans, along with a packed gallery of on-the-spot spectators, cheer, bet, and keep score as finalists are chosen and a "lucky" young woman is named Miss America. This sophisticated sideshow computes talent and feminine charm as the contestants approach the microphone one by one with practiced stride. Flawlessly groomed, they purr out with carefully coached diction a mechanical sentence about themselves and their aspirations.

Money, of course, sparks the real scramble for the sweepstakes. "I want to be a doctor—or a court judge—or a professional performer. . . ." If young men who aspire to these heights were to compete in this fashion, Americans would probably shrug it off with a ho-hum, so-what's-new? attitude. Doesn't everybody want to be something terrific?

Women in America have convinced the world—including Americans—that we are a race of royalty. The American woman of the closing decades of this century holds in her grasp the choicest morsels in history—opportunities of every description. She is armed with legal rights, social standing, limitless educational choices, and the comfortable elbow room of leisure time. But it is never enough. Sociologist Jessie Barnard, in an end-of-the-year wrap-up in a national magazine, bemoaned:

> . . . women have been left sort of bereaved, psychologically left high and dry. They don't even get the support they need from their husbands. Wives give emotional support to husbands twice as much as husbands give to wives. . . suffer severe emotional deprivation. The mental health of women, especially of housewives, is what I have called the No. 1 public health problem in this country.[1]

Step into my mental workshop where I have been tinkering for years with a balanced view of God's woman. I have chiseled out old thoughts, tried on new ideas, patched a premise here and there, and actually discarded some old rusty arguments. I used to believe, for example, that women really were the weaker sex.

I am not the first mortal ever to have undertaken such a project. Numbers of treatises on "how to live with yourself though female" have surfaced. Thousands of thinkers have mulled over the pieces of the puzzle. Just accept the fragments that we have, some say. You can never really be balanced, so ignore as much as you can and God will give you the grace to put up with what hangs over.

But that sitting-down stuff is old-fashioned. We are in a bootstrap society. Nowadays our world believes, "You only go 'round once in life and you gotta grab for all the gusto you can get!" Like the dog on the bridge!

The Woman in Progress

A gold nugget is tucked away in the wisdom literature of the Old Testament; many think it is God's formula for the true essence of womanhood. It is neatly packaged in the final twenty-one verses of the book of Proverbs. Actually, in the Hebrew it forms an acrostic with each of the verses beginning with a successive letter of the Hebrew alphabet. Apparently it was intended to be memorized and this was a memory tool.

The chapter came from the pen of one of Israel's kings—possibly Solomon. He is quoting his mother and so the viewpoint is feminine; from a woman about a woman. In Jewish custom, fathers taught sons; but throughout the book of Proverbs the mother is also mentioned as a teacher.

Motherly Reminders

I have two sons. Believe me, my choicest advice goes to them. It's occasionally my privilege to counsel other young men, especially concerning women. I *am* one; I've lived with them; I know them. When it comes to my own sons, you can be sure I'll give them the straight scoop. I have their best interests at heart. So it was, I believe, with this mother in Proverbs 31. She begins, however, by waving a red flag, a threefold warning. Two are negative; one is positive.

(1) Don't pursue indiscriminate liaisons with women; these relationships will weaken you as a ruler and responsible leader. I know exactly what she meant. Busy little bumblebees have rung our telephone to speak with my young sons. Personally, I never called a young man on the phone. During my adolescence, little ladies just were not allowed to be that aggressive.

Of course, it wasn't because I didn't think about it. I can remember one luckless young man whose picture I snapped with my brownie camera. His sister and I became "good" friends and I wanted him to notice me so badly that I finally even wangled an overnight invitation to their home. Think of it! Breakfast with *him*. Would you believe I didn't see him? He never ate breakfast with the family because he had a job delivering papers early in the morning. He didn't get back before I had to leave!

Do not give your strength to women. . . ." You'll get stung, says this momma. She knew the female instinct for tapping into a prestigious, attractive man. Watch your step, son. Admit it; we women can be wily and wicked, and we can cover it all up with beauty and charm. What are little girls made of? "Sugar and spice and everything nice"? Not all of them. For some that's just their icing and it should read: "Deceit and dice, and a very high price"!

(2) Avoid strong drink; that's for weak and dying people. You must be a clear-headed administrator; you cannot afford to make mistakes.

(3) Take care of the poor people, the "down and outers." A righteous judge takes care of those who cannot help themselves. Jesus Christ echoed this same thought when he talked about the privilege of giving.

Royal Ideal of a Woman

With this frontispiece, the queen mother now unveils her literary photograph of the ideal woman. It is a composite picture: one shot is through the lens of interpersonal relationships; another catches the viewpoint of her husband; a wide-angle view examines her various interests; a close-up reveals processes she uses to accomplish her goals; and an interior view uncovers her motives and attitudes.

Note the flow of movement. Perhaps it is a clue to her priorities. She progresses from her husband to her household to her community. The section closes with a short editorial.

Who can find a virtuous woman?
   For her price is far above rubies.
The heart of her husband doth safely trust in her so that
   he shall have no need of spoil.
She will do him good and not evil all the days of her
   life.
She seeketh wool, and flax and worketh willingly with
   her hands.
She is like the merchants' ships;
   She bringeth her food from afar.
She riseth also while it is yet night,
    And giveth meat to her household,
    and a portion to her maidens.
She considereth a field, and buyeth it;
    With the fruit of her hands she planteth a vineyard.
She girdeth her loins with strength,
    and strengtheneth her arms.
    She perceiveth that her merchandise is good:
Her candle goeth not out by night.
    She layeth her hands to the spindle,
    and her hands hold the distaff.

She stretcheth out her hand to the poor;
  Yea, she reacheth forth her hands to the needy.
She is not afraid of the snow for her household:
  For all her household are clothed with scarlet.
She maketh herself coverings of tapestry;
  Her clothing is silk and purple.
Her husband is known in the gates,
  When he sitteth among the elders of the land.
She maketh fine linen, and selleth it;
  And delivereth girdles unto the merchant.
Strength and honor are her clothing;
  And she shall rejoice in time to come.
She openeth her mouth with wisdom;
  And in her tongue is the law of kindness.
She looketh well to the ways of her household,
  And eateth not the bread of idleness.
Her children arise up, and call her blessed;
  Her husband also, and he praiseth her.
Many daughters have done virtuously,
  But thou excellest them all.
  Favor is deceitful and beauty is vain,
    But a woman that feareth the Lord, she shall
      be praised.
Give her of the fruit of her hands;
  And let her own works praise her in the gates.

                   (Prov. 31:10–31, KJV)

Many women have told me they come away from this chapter out of breath or tired or with a terrible inferiority complex. It jumps up and grabs us! We can't help but notice all the textiles she processed, the food she prepared, and the way she took care of herself and those around her. She worked, even though she was affluent. I remember reading in Sam Levinson's delightful recollections, entitled *In One Era And Out The Other*, "We had a permissive father; he permitted us to work."[2] Leisure time did not seem to be one of this woman's concerns.

The opening question is rhetorical. "Who can find a virtuous woman," or it can be translated "a noble wife." The question implies that every man is looking for one. The answer? She is extremely rare; rare as rubies. Remember this was before the discovery of the diamond mines in Africa. We think of rubies as being the corundum gem from the Far East. The blue corundum is the familiar blue sapphire, and the blood red ruby is even more valuable. Recently, however, scholars have come to feel that this "ruby" could be coral, which was highly prized in ancient times.

Several years ago, *National Geographic* magazine carried a fascinating article by Dr. Eugenie Clark, called "The Strangest Sea."

The Red Sea is perhaps the most extraordinary large body Barrieof water on the earth. It has a higher salinity than any other ocean. No rivers run into it. . . . Most ocean depths are cold, but . . . in certain volcanic depths temperatures reach 138°F. . . . fortunes of immeasurable worth . . . iron, manganese, lead, gold, silver, copper, zinc—estimated in the billions of dollars. At the northern shore—where the Gulf of Suez and the Gulf of Aquaba meet—here barren desert drops into blue tropical water harboring incredibly beautiful coral reefs. . . . Here, as in certain other Red Sea areas, the profusion of different corals exceeds that of any known comparable area—even the Great Barrier Reef of Australia.[3]

The pictures which accompany this article bear captions such as "brilliant red gorgonian coral" and "coral of such brilliant red as to be indescribable." Whatever the actual gem, only a very few could afford such an investment and this woman is said to be *far above* even that—priceless!

How She Treats Her Man

The first qualification concerns the woman's husband. We learn from the context that he was an astute, intelligent, and respected man of the world. Imagine this caliber of man—apparently urbane, sophisticated, and successful—who *fully trusted* this woman in every respect, no questions asked. She was some kind of woman!

It's very important to recognize this passage is *not* about the husband-wife relationship *per se.* In the ancient cultures, almost every woman was married. She would be the member of a harem, or under Jewish law she could be a widow placed under the care of her husband's brother after his death. Every woman was somehow assigned to a husband; there was no other way of financial support. The thrust of the statement is that her character caused him to respond with trust.

Western women today are so programmed in the game of "how to win and hold a man" we forget that in those days women did not manipulate men. When a man believed in a woman, she had earned his confidence. "That's very nice," we quip with a turn of the head while our slow sarcastic eyelids flutter. "Like looking through the glass at a rare specimen in a museum," we say. "It sure would be nice to have, but it's out of my class." No it isn't, really.

Modern marriage psychologists have done a lot of dissecting to find out what is the best recipe for first-rate togetherness. Under the heading of something they call "self-other fulfillment," they have laid out eight ingredients which are named "basic heart hungers": security, service, esteem, enjoyment, love, limits, freedom, and faith. "Marital partners become key resource persons for supplying the basic foods of the spirit. Each spouse has considerable power to nourish or to starve the other's personality."[4]

That's my checklist and it will keep me busy for a lifetime. When I am generating these factors, as well as receiving them, there is fantastic and fabulous matrimony. Here's how it works. My husband of twenty years comes home tired, drooping with discouragement. (At least, I think that's why his eyelids are hanging down on the sides.) I have a report to give on our teen-aged son which must be made and I can forecast the weather in our house will probably be stormy. "Lord," I'm praying inside, "lend me your umbrella. I'm going to need it."

But first, I focus on him. A chance to change clothes, a cool drink, a few words of sincere concern, and minutes of listening. Then the problem. I can't put it off; it's urgent. But my words, my tone of voice, my face can package that problem in a wrapping that says, "Here, honey, we have to share this matter." And when it is shared, my self-control and my love for everybody involved can ease or intensify the pain.

This Proverbs woman could live in today's world with or without a husband. If God gives her a husband, this is descriptive of his response, but the point is that her character is honest, reliable, and capable. She is a long-term, blue-chip investment.

Her husband would have "no need of spoil"; that is, no lack of gain. From her enterprises the entire family benefitted. She planned; she had projects; she was a mover, moving the family upward in the socio-economic scale of her community.

What? I thought Christians were supposed to be poor. Isn't poverty next to cleanliness, after godliness? No, the New Testament commends us for being poor *in spirit*. It is an attitude of heart, with a positive and a negative: priorities and a clear lack of anxiety. Know what's important. Do that first and then stop worrying (Matt. 6:33).

God may use poverty to teach us to depend on Him, but the overall picture in the Bible is abundance for all His creatures. I have a friend who is chronically in debt. She's more concerned about what her friends think of her house and clothes than how much she owes her creditors.

The book of Hebrews reminds us that Moses made a tough decision. He "esteemed the reproaches of Christ greater than the riches of Egypt." Many of Christ's disciples left lucrative businesses to gain something far better. "What will a man be profited," asked our Lord, "if he gains the whole world, and forfeits his soul? . . ." (Matt. 16:26).

Christ taught His own to keep a very light hold on material possessions. "So therefore, no one of you can be My disciple who does not give up all his own possessions" (Luke 14:33). It must be an individual choice made through faith. The rich young ruler was not condemned because of his wealth; rather, Jesus focused on "one thing you still lack." The problem was with his choice of material possession over spiritual life. It is not what we have; it is how we hold it. "Beware, and be on your guard against every form of greed," warned the Lord, "for not even when one has an abundance does his life consist of his possessions" (Luke 12:15). Proverbs teaches it is honoring to God to *have* and *properly utilize* this world's goods.

How She Kept "Shoes on the Kids"

This ideal woman developed her talents; she was alert, aware, and alive. She "seeks wool and flax"; that is, she made sure there is ample available. These were the two staple raw textiles; wool for the winter clothing, and flax for the linen summer wear.

Wool was abundant in Palestine. Historically it was a top-notch fabric because of its resilience, wrinkle-resistance, felting qualities, low heat conductivity, elasticity, and warmth. It was, and has been ever since, an indispensable article of war. In fact, no fibre has ever been discovered with properties equal to it for clothing armies. It is hygienic and durable. In modern warfare it is used for felt washers for shells, guns, submarine and airplane engines, torpedoes, tanks, and more. In this ancient time it would have been used possibly in the shields, spears, helmets, and armor. It is estimated that a soldier's equipment and clothing use four to ten times as much wool as a civilian's. Remember, Israel was chronically at war.

At home it was winter clothing, and she processed this willingly—"pleasurably". What did she enjoy so much? Carding, backwashing, oiling to prevent brittleness, sometimes gilling to straighten fibres, combing, sometimes recombing, then spinning and weaving with no spinning wheels.

Wait a minute! You're protesting. "She didn't do all that by herself!" No, undoubtedly she had servants. Nevertheless, the text says she *worked willingly with her hands*. In fact, the word "hand(s)" is used ten times in these twenty-one verses. She was physically involved in the process and also probably had to train, supervise, and patiently oversee the whole operation.

In the summer there was flax to prepare. It was a long, tedious process. The deseeded straw had to be retted (partly rotted) to dissolve the gums that bound the fibres to the woody portion of the stem. The common method was to spread straw out evenly and thinly on the ground, usually on grassland, where it was subjected to weathering and the action of soil-borne bacteria. After seven to twenty-one days, the bark could be loosened and peeled off. Then the straw was gathered and set in shocks to dry. The fibre was separated from the woody core by breaking and scutching, usually accomplished by passing the straw between fluted rolls or crushing them between slatted, hand-breaking frames. The scutched fibre would then be ready for spinning. It had to be hackled (combed) and twisted into yarn. The long fibres made the finest yarns, while the short, tangled ones were used for coarse fabrics—twine, cord, and rope. Don't forget the seeds, too, which were used for linseed oil.

In sharp contrast, I couldn't help but think of a poem I saw in the *Saturday Evening Post*. It was called, "Busy, Busy, Busy Day!" It demonstrates how far out of it we really are today.

> I've gone for a drink and sharpened my pencils
> Searched through my desk for forgotten utensils,
> Reset my watch and adjusted my chair,
> Loosened my tie and straightened my hair,
> Emptied the wastebasket, filled the carafe
> Sorted the paper clips, opened the safe,
> Filled my pen and tested the blotter,
> Gone for another drink of water,
> Adjusted the calendar, raised the blinds,
> Sorted erasers of different kinds.
> Now, down to work I can finally sit.
> Oops! Too late. It's time to quit![5]

Admittedly, that's a bit tongue-in-cheek. But I used to work for the U.S. government, and I assure you, I can identify with this poem.

Back to our perpetual-motion gal, we find her now in the madding crowd of the market. It seems she was not content with squash from her own backyard. She probably bartered home-grown products for imported spices and delicacies which arrived on merchant ships from the Mediterranean Sea. The idea is not only distance, but quality. She shopped for the best buys. (Smart homemakers have *always* done that!)

A parody on Shakespeare tugs at the heartstrings of the grocery shopper with inflation puffing at the prices.

To buy or not to buy; that is the question:
Whether 'tis wiser in the end to suffer
The hurt and havoc of outrageous prices,
Or to take arms against the costs of groceries,
And by a boycott end them. To Plant; to reap;
No more; and by our planting say we end
The monstrous charges and the rippings-off
We've all been heir to. 'Tis a consummation
Devoutly to be wished. To plant; to reap;
To reap; perchance to *fail*—ay, there's the rub,
For from our purple thumbs what weeds may come,
When we have tilled the soil and sowed the seed,
Must give us pause; there's the respect
That makes calamity of buying food;
For who would pay their crazy asking price:
A pot o' gold to fill the bowl with fruit,
A fortune for some simple salad greens,
When he himself might his own larder fill
With a mere trowel? Who would dollars bear
Grunting and sweating, to the checkout stand.
But that the dread of laboring in the yard,
Day after day, week after weary week—
To bring forth crabgrass, petrifies the will,
And makes us rather buy the stuff we need
Than take the chance of growing it ourselves.
Thus doubting does make suckers of us all,
And thus the mundane need to feed the face
Sends us like sheep to supermarket shelves
And find us paying-paying through the nose.[6]

How She Directed the Domestic Traffic

"She riseth while it is yet night"—a phrase to undo
the later riser. She utilized the early hours of the day to
facilitate and to plan for others. Early morning is a great
time to design the day. It's quite obvious this little
woman was a domestic engineer who had a daily
blueprint; that's why she got so much accomplished.

What did this up-before-the-sun mean to her personally? It meant inconvenience, a private price she
paid to minister to her maidens. Usually people who
have hired help let them get up and serve the master
and the mistress. Not here. This woman had a servant
heart, which is one of the marks of a great leader.

One of our own great leaders, the distinguished Sen.
Mark Hatfield, was seen not long ago stacking chairs
after a breakfast meeting. In just minutes he was due at
a Senate committee meeting where he was the ranking
member. He could have asked any number of bystand-
ers to perform that menial task, but he has the servant
heart of a Christian leader.

Christ is our supreme leader, who cares more about
those under Him than they care about Him. This same
spirit emanates from the woman in Proverbs. No wonder she garnered a unanimous vote of approval!

She cared and she showed it.

Our heroine now has a project with a purpose. It's
not just busy work, nor was she speculating in real
estate with her extra dividends. She "considereth a
field . . . planteth a vineyard." According to 1 Kings,
every complete Jewish home included a vineyard.
Wine growers in California and Europe tell us that fine
wines must be produced under precise conditions—
just the right water, sun, cold, and drainage. She had to

know some technical information in order to buy wisely and develop one from scratch.

The money she was investing in this venture, remember, was her own earnings ("with the fruit of her hands"), possibly gained from selling custom-made garments to get the new project going. She did not necessarily do all the labor herself, but again, she had to oversee. She started with a fallow field; she had to see the potential, to use supervisory expertise, to direct the planting, the nurturing, the processing, and the selling. She was an executive in every sense.

Should women be in business and professions? Of course they should. The question hinges on their motives, their attitudes, their function in the culture.

"Involvement" seems to be the word that fits this "virtuous woman." She "girdeth her loins." Historians suggest that this description explains the process of wrapping the skirt tightly around the legs to facilitate laborious work. She did not allow herself to be a lady of leisure and wear loose, flowing robes. Even though she was a woman of means, perhaps even royalty, she was right in the middle of things, working and enjoying every minute of it.

Benjamin Franklin once wrote about laborers:

> When men are employed they are best contented, for on the days they worked they were good-natured and cheerful, and with the consciousness of having done a good day's work, they spent the evening jollily, but on . . . idle days they were mutinous and quarrelsome. . . .[7]

Her Self-Improvement Program

In the same verse with the hard work is a reference to "strengthening her arm." Whatever the exact meaning, it seems she took care of her physical body. She was not a worried, frazzled, defensive housewife who sacrificed herself on the altar of domesticity.

Right here in the middle of this bright, cheerful description of God's ideal woman, let's hold our fingers in the page and flip over to a dreadful prophecy by Isaiah. Apparently the women of Judah reacted to work just about the same way many American women do. In their prosperity they turned to themselves. It seems appropriate to remind ourselves here of God's ghastly indictment:

> Next, he will judge the haughty Jewish women, who mince along, noses in the air, tinkling bracelets on their ankles, with wanton eyes that rove among the crowds to catch the glances of the men. The Lord will send a plague of scabs to ornament their heads! He will expose their nakedness for all to see. No longer shall they tinkle with self-assurance as they walk. For the Lord will strip away their artful beauty and their ornaments, their necklaces and bracelets and veils of shimmering gauze. Gone shall be their scarves and ankle chains, headbands, earrings, and perfumes; their rings and jewels, and party clothes and negligees and capes and ornate combs and purses; their mirrors, lovely lingerie, beautiful dresses and veils. Instead of smelling of sweet perfume, they'll stink; for sashes they'll use ropes; their well-set hair will all fall out; they'll wear sacks instead of robes.
>
> All their beauty will be gone; all that will be left to them is shame and disgrace. Their husbands shall die in battle; the women, ravaged, shall sit crying on the ground (Isa. 3:16–26, TLB).

Little Bit of Business

Back to the script. Our lovely woman displayed judgment and discernment. She *perceived* that her merchandise was good. She was a professional seamstress and nutritionist who knew quality. With a practiced eye she sought not a cheap bargain, but excellence and goodness in her purchases.

At night, her "lamp goeth not out." How in the world did she get enough sleep? Good news. In the ancient East, a lamp burned in the home of citizens of means to signify their availability. Here was a haven for the distressed. The old Bedouins had a saying, "He sleeps in darkness," which conveyed the idea of living in abject poverty. A burning candle signified prosperity.

The spindle and the distaff were tools of the day— two flat, circular objects used to work textile fibers. The functions are not clear, but this good wife used them to help provide for the less fortunate. Christ reminds us "the poor you have with you always" (Matt. 26:11). There is never any excuse for loneliness. Somebody always needs help. She "stretched her hand to the poor," responding to calls for help. She also "reaches forth," taking the initiative. The word for "hand" in verse 19 means "fingers," and in verse 20 it means "palm." The idea is both active and passive. She gave when she was asked, and she offered when she was not asked.

The "strength and dignity" is indicative of strong financial posture and the resultant esteem. Personal security and a sense of well-being is what we all want—insurance against the cold snaps. Her cold front came swooping down from the mountains much like our blue Texas northers come whistling across the plains from the Rocky Mountains. All the provisions were in; all the preparations were made. "Scarlet" was not a color, but a heavy, luxurious fabric. By extension, it could also connote her emotional and spiritual clothing. She does not just have the minimum; rather, she has completely adequate covering.

The prophet Jeremiah (17:7–8) refers to the man who trusts in the Lord as being prepared. He says he will be like a tree planted by the water, "that extends its roots by a stream and will not fear when the heat comes; but its leaves will be green, and it will not be anxious in a year of drought nor cease to yield fruit." The heat will come; the drought is certain; but it's no problem when you are prepared.

Along with everything else, this lady also had a first-class designer's wardrobe. Her garments were regal, imported, custom-made. Her high standard of living related to her husband's position. He was a leading citizen and she was an asset to him. His importance and influence were undoubtedly due, at least in part, to her support. Apparently she had no illusions of grandeur; she had herself in perspective. Money and position had not turned her head.

As a craftsman, she excelled. The "girdles" were elaborately embroidered sashes which she apparently wore as well as sold. "Strength and honor" trotted along beside her shrewd business acumen. That is, she had a stable, honest reputation—a high esteem that foreshadowed future happiness. She was making friends and laying away for the future a wealth of resources which would bring joy in her senior years.

When She Speaks

We hear her speaking, and "in her tongue is the law of kindness." Lest we think of her as a sharp-tongued, beady-eyed female haberdasher, the writer describes her manner of speech. Good sense and discretion prevail; she is not officious nor domineering, even though in our terms she would probably be the female VIP "beautiful person" who lived in the big house on the hill. She was apparently gentle and compassionate as she spoke, and her care of details in her home precluded any move in the direction of laziness.

Those nearest to her—in her case her husband and children—spontaneously cheer her on. They "rise up" and call her blessed. The Hebrew word is the simple phrase for getting up in the morning. Every day they open their eyes, feeling glad she belongs to them. Do those under our roofs feel that way about us?

Let me give a personal testimony. It's soon going to be thirty years since I walked in white down that center aisle in a little church, and stepped into a world much bigger than I ever imagined. My bridegroom was a smiling student in a graduate school of theology.

Like a kernel of popcorn in hot oil, he soon started to explode. He was into just about everything young ministers do. And everything he did was with tireless zeal and fierce intensity, including loving his wife. Although he criticized, condemned, and complained (That's the three-part no-no in Dale Carnegie's *How To Win Friends* . . .) about everything from my housekeeping to my hairdos, he loved me with equal gusto. Frustrating but fulfilling—even fun! And funny, too. He had a formidable sense of humor that teased and sometimes tormented my struggling self-esteem. Discouraging, but never dull! I sometimes think that a good visual aid of my psyche would be hammered aluminum. But his hammer blows were not only censures, but love and praise. If I bombed out with a meal, I "faced the music," but when I served a winner, there was loud and sincere tribute.

He appreciates me, and he tells the world until sometimes I'm embarrassed. But you know what it does to me? It's like a blast from a jet engine. I'd do anything to please that one who loves me.

What prompts praise? Certainly you've got to be more than a good cook. I would suggest—and this zooms right back to my gr-r-eat-grandmother in the Garden of Eden—that a wife must fill up the empty spaces in her man's life. This includes not only his stomach, but also all those many emotional and psychological places nobody else even knows are empty. Only the sensor of selfless love can spot those places. Only with the insight of deep caring can they be heard and seen and felt.

Her husband praises her. Any wife can attest that this is the sweetest music of matrimony. He tells her she is the greatest. Nothing motivates a woman more than that!

The inspired commentary at the end is the summation and interpretation, lest the reader get bedazzled by the thin air in the high altitude of the chapter. Yes, grace and beauty are there—natural gifts, no doubt. But the part that is really permanent and noteworthy is the character of godliness and that must be developed.

Are you walking into God's beauty parlor today and saying, I want to be like the girl there in that picture, that word picture in Proverbs 31?

Okay, He answers, but it's going to take a real do-over. First, we'll have to cut off that straggly streak of laziness that holds you back. We'll have to de-emphasize that long, pointy tongue that gets you into so much trouble. We'll have to put you on a diet of de-fatted service to other people and exercise those flabby prayer muscles.

God wants to write a sequel to Proverbs 31 with you in mind. He has already given us the pattern to follow and has also furnished us with the "how to." "If any man is in Christ, he is a new creature; the old things passed away; behold, new things have come" (2 Cor. 5:17).

Newness in God's eyes comes only through His Son, through becoming a member of God's family by faith.

"As many as received Him, to them He gave the right to become children of God, even to those who believe in His name" (John 1:12).

Don't lash yourself for not being able to transform everything immediately. Start with the essentials: life in Christ, then growth and development in His Word. ". . . the testimony of the Lord is sure, making wise the simple" (Ps. 19:7).

Study Questions: Chapter 9

"We are rushing to go to a reception, but I have to stop and search for the mislaid address and I can't find my gloves. Halfway down the block I notice a run in my stocking. Patiently my husband turns back, waits with the motor running while I rush inside to change. And when I return, breathless, he leans over, and says, 'Relax, honey, you're worth waiting for.' My heart leaps up in a little prayer of gratitude to God for being cherished."*

Pull a page out of your own life. Select a typical day. Write down everything you did from the time you got up until you went to bed. Now review it and check the places where the woman of Proverbs 31 would have acted differently (given your circumstances.) Make a list of changes you need to make. Now pray and ask God to show you how to make those changes.

*(Marjorie Holmes Mighell, *I've Got to Talk to Somebody, God.* Doubleday & Co.)

Footnotes

Chapter 1

1. Margaret L. Coit, "The Sweep Westward," *The Life History of the United States*, vol. 4, (New York: Time-Life Books 1963), p. 88.

2. Paula Stern, *Atlantic*, March, 1970.

3. Cited by John Bartlette, *Familiar Quotations*, (Boston: Little, Brown and Co., 1955), p. 728.

4. Francis Schaeffer, *Genesis in Space and Time* (Downers Grove, Ill.: Inter-Varsity Press; Glendale, Calif.: Regal Books, 1972), p. 46.

5. C. I. Scofield, D.D., ed., *The New Scofield Reference Bible* (New York: Oxford University Press, 1967), p. 6.

6. Edward J. Young, *Genesis 3* (London: Banner of Truth Trust, 1966), p. 67.

7. Dr. Roy Zuck, *Barb Please Wake Up* (Wheaton, Ill.: Victor Books), p. 16.

8. Elisabeth Elliot, *Let Me Be A Woman* (Wheaton, Ill.: Tyndale House, Inc., 1976), p. 185.

Chapter 2

1. Carl E. Williams and John F. Crosby, eds., *Choice*

and Challenge: Contemporary Readings in Marriage (Bloomington, Ind.: Indiana University, 1974).

2. R. K. Harrison, "The World of Genesis and the Patriarch," *Zondervan Pictorial Bible Atlas*, E. M. Blaiklock, ed. (Grand Rapids: Zondervan Publishing Co., 1969), p. 48.

3. Dr. Alexander Whyte, *Bible Characters* (Grand Rapids: Zondervan Publishing Co., 1952).

4. Rollo May, *Love and Will* (New York: Dell Publishing Co., Inc., 1969), p. 29.

5. Lois Wyse, "Love Poems For the Very Married," cited by Howard and Charlotte Clinebell, *The Intimate Marriage* (New York: Harper and Row, 1970), p. 27.

Chapter 3

1. Marilyn Siegel Smith, "Commencement Ceremonies," *Harvard Today* (Harvard Law School) June 17, 1976.

2. B. F. Skinner interviewed by Wm. F. Buckley, "Firing Line," EKERA-TV, Dallas, Texas, aired Nov. 4, 1973.

3. Benjamin Spock, M.D., "Taking Care of a Child and a Home: An Honorable Profession for Men and Women," *Redbook*. April, 1976. p. 22.

Chapter 4

1. Carl Rowan, *Dallas Morning News* (Syndicated Column, Field Enterprises, Inc.) Sept. 13, 1976.

2. Corrie ten Boom, *Prison Letters* (Old Tappan, N.J.: Fleming Revell Co., 1975) see introduction.

Chapter 5

1. Letter published in a syndicated column by Dr. Joyce Brothers (Bell McClure Syndicate) Oct. 4, 1968.

2. Dr. Otto Sperling quoted by Harriet LaBarre,

"The Sexually Sensible Woman," *Ladies Home Journal*, 1971.

3. Alida Greydanus, "Matters of the Heart," *Saturday Review*, April 3, 1976, p. 6.

Chapter 6

1. Corrie ten Boom, *The Hiding Place*, (Old Tappan, N.J.: Fleming H. Revell Co., 1971) see introduction.

2. Bernard Goldman, "Politicking in Ancient Persia," *Natural History*, April, 1976, p. 36.

3. Corrie ten Boom, *Hiding Place*.

4. Samuel Eliot Morison, *Admiral of the Ocean Sea*, Vol. 1 (Boston: Little, Brown and Co.; reprinted by Time, Inc. Book Division, 1962) p. 203.

5. *Ibid.*

6. *Ibid.*, p. 188.

Chapter 7

1. Axel Ingelman Sundberg, *A Child Is Born* (New York: Dell Publishing Co. Inc., 1965), p. 85.

Chapter 8

1. Quoted by John Bartlett, *Familiar Quotations* (Boston: Little, Brown and Co., 1955), p. 813.

Chapter 9

1. Jessie Barnard, *U.S. News and World Report*, Dec. 8, 1975.

2. Sam Levinson, *In One Era and Out the Other*, (New York: Simon and Schuster), p. 23.

3. Dr. Eugene Clark, "The Strangest Sea," *National Geographic*, Sept., 1975, pp. 342–61.

4. Howard J. and Charlotte Clinebell, *The Intimate Marriage* (New York: Harper and Row, 1970), p. 84.

5. Leonard A. Paris, "Busy, Busy, Busy Day!" *Saturday Evening Post*, March, 1975, p. 69.

6. Lillian E. Carlton "Shakespeare on Inflation," *Saturday Evening Post*, March, 1975, p. 69.

7. *The Autobiography of Benjamin Franklin* (New York: Random House, 1944), p. 167.